The (other) *F* Word

The (other) F Word

Faith, the Last Taboo

By Steve Maltz

SAFFRON PLANET

Saffron Planet
PO Box 2215
Ilford IG1 9TR
UK
T: +44 (0) 208 551 1719
E: contact@saffronplanet.net
W: www.sppublishing.com

ISBN 978-0-9562296-3-2

Typeset by **documen**, www.documen.co.uk
Cover design by Phil Maltz
Printed and bound by CPI Group (UK) Ltd, Croydon, CR0 4YY

"Faith is reason grown courageous."

Sherwood Eddy

Special thanks to Chris, Peter, Simon, Howard, Jony and Kit for wise promptings, Kevin and countless others for wise advice, Jackie for weaving your usual magic over the words and Monica, just for being there.

CONTENTS

Introduction

We live in uncertain times. We seek control of our lives where possible but are faced with the gradual encroachment of uncertainty, in the guise of domestic terrorism, quirks of climate and economic shakes and rattles. Science suggests that it holds the solutions, yet has failed to deliver. Ditto to politics, ditto to philosophy, ditto to religion. Yet each can boast cast-iron theories that offer salvation, safety and security for all. What's gone wrong, then...?

Simple answer... it's you and I that have gone wrong. The tools of science, the ideas of politics and philosophy and the teachings of religion may have the potential to cure all of the ills of this World, but all fall short because each requires "little old us" to pass from theory to practice, from imagination to application. If we were just honest enough to admit it, our hands are tainted by our human failings, our ambitions, our pride, our misguided endeavours and our hunger for fame and fortune. Putting it simply, we just can't be trusted to create a World fit for all. History is a witness to this great failing. There's something that's just not right in the heart of man.

> *"Our scientific power has outrun our spiritual power. We have guided missiles and misguided men".*
>
> *Martin Luther King Jr.*

I state my case up front. I offer no sincere subterfuge or hidden agendas. I believe that man (and woman) alone is incapable of ordering the World for the good of all. We're pretty good at looking after the needs of ourselves, our families and friends and those with whom we identify. But our horizons are limited, the vast bulk of humanity lays beyond, out of sight, out of mind. Perhaps you agree with me, perhaps you don't. Perhaps you're willing to discuss this further, secure within your own safe boundaries.

I believe that our World is broken and uncertain because it has lost touch with its Source, its Creator, the misunderstood and maligned One who formed man from the dust of the ground and breathed life into him. Like fingernails scraped across a chalkboard, or the screech of a stylus across vinyl, I have condemned myself to ridicule from most quarters. I have apparently nailed my "God delusion" to the mast of a sinking ship, as the cuckoo chimes madness o'clock.

Hasn't God been disproved by the media intelligencia, the chattering classes, the opinionated bloggerati and the Dawkinites? Apparently so, but there are some of us who believe that He's very much alive and kicking, larger than life and ready to "kick ass".

Did you know that in our country there have been times when the existence of God was a given for the majority of the population? Even just seventy years ago, when King George VI called the nation to prayer during WW2, the majority complied and packed the churches. Some may have been hedging their bets, but most had some sort of grasp of some sort of concept of a supernatural Being. Yet if the current royals were to repeat this call, any serious response would be a comparative trickle, with the rest made up of the curious, the cynical and the devout of other faiths.

Our nation has changed. It has changed in many ways and it is my contention that these changes have gone unnoticed. Our mindsets have shifted by stealth, driven by forces beyond ourselves that can be traced to ideas going back over many hundreds of years. There is nothing new under the sun and it is vital that every thinking person should be presented with the full facts in historical context, rather than be swayed by the forked tongues of the media commentators, who make a very nice living out of contrariness and bucket-loads of attractively written personal opinion.

We suffer from information-overload these days; There is little room for the mind to breath, choked by the dense rhetoric from the web, the print media, radio and TV. It is time you stopped for a moment, took a long deep breath… and opened your minds to *alternative* possibilities.

It ain't cool to believe in God, unless it is a God of our own imaginings, constructed for convenience from shards and slivers of quasi-beliefs that float about in our collective consciousness. Many say they believe in God, but few would tie their beliefs down into a set of dogmas and creeds. Instead they construct a divine photo-fit that usually bears an uncanny resemblance to their own expectations – *if there was a God, here's how I think he would operate.*

So is God whatever we want Him to be or is He a real, objective, living, spiritual Being? He is either one or the other. If He is the former, then it's all comfortably harmless and we all live in our personal cocoons, sustained by our unique beliefs. If He is the latter, then there could be an awful lot of people out there who are making a *really big mistake*, one that could have extreme consequences.

I ask you to hear me out. You've heard the usual party-line. Our media is currently awash with the mutterings of the atheists, with their priestly classes and hierarchy of spokespeople. My guess is that all you've heard of the *alternative* is through hearsay, or half forgotten memories, or from the misguided lives and proclamations of certain "men of the cloth", or through the many distorted parodies paraded through dramas, soaps and sitcoms.

Yes, the *alternative* has admittedly had a chequered history, much that is shameful, wicked and downright wrong. That is undeniable and history is not going to be rewritten here to airbrush out the "inconvenient truths". Instead I return to my early assertion, that we humans tend to ruin everything we get our hands on.

God, whether we believe in Him or not, should not be blamed for our shortcomings. Instead it is time we had a good hard look at ourselves and the way we see the World.

Many of you will agree with me if I say that the World can be a rotten place, that the outlook for mankind is not good, that religion can be an ugly thing and that most of us are quite frightened about the future. But how many of you are willing to concede that not only does God exist, but that He cares about us and can provide some answers to the problems of our World?

It is time to hear the case for the Divine defence.

1

I Believe
(or Perhaps Not)

IIIIIIIIIIIIIIIIIIIIIIIIIIIIIIIIIIIIIIIIIIIIIIIIIIIIIIIIIIIIIIIIIIIIIIIIIIIIIIIIIIIIIIIIIIIIIIIIIIIIIIIIIIIIIIIIIIII

(An imagined conversation between
God and mankind)

God speaks
Why don't you believe in me?

Mankind proclaims
You have no relevance to us.

God answers
Just because you live in a society that has decided to do
without me, it doesn't mean that you have to go along with
everything that is thrown at you. Any student of history
would know that a predominant feature of your society is
the rise of individualism at the expense of the community,
from extended families to bedsits and loft apartments, from
Sunday church to Sunday lie-ins. Yet you are not truly
independent, even though you think you are. There's a part

of you that needs to be connected and, if that is not to me, then it will be to something else.

You laugh at my true followers as deluded individuals voluntarily binding themselves to rules and regulations, but are you any different, I ask you? *No man is an island*, someone once said, and this is truer than you think. You may consider me an irrelevance, but you are very relevant to me; you have always been very special to me. But this you have forgotten. Yet there's a part of you that is seeking me, a homing device buried deep within you in spiritual places you probably don't even know exist. Some of you are aware of this and do seek me. A few find me, but most are deflected on their journey and either think they've found me or settle for alternatives.

Ask yourselves why the ardent atheists out there are so sure that I don't exist that they are happy to spend a large part of their lives telling this to all who are happy to listen to them. As with every other human being, they have this unconscious desire to be connected to me. Let us call this *the Longing*. But their life journey has marred this desire. Perhaps they have been let down by one of my followers, or have parents who deny my existence, or maybe they just haven't been paying attention. They still have *the Longing* but instead of recognising its source they satisfy it in their own way with science, philosophy, politics or any other human endeavour borne from the mind of man. *The Longing* has been redirected, as it has by all who answer it with products of their own cleverness, or even with the claims of rival gods.

Mankind proclaims
We just don't like you.

God answers
Hey, I'm not out to win any popularity contests. If I am who I say I am, then perhaps it's you who should look out. If you don't like me, then at least it's a step up from not actually believing in me. But if you have made this step, then you must consider the consequences. Unless I am a god that you have made up, a god made in your own image, a pet deity, then I must be the God who created you, who has the whole affairs of the World in his hand. In which case, perhaps you should be more concerned with *whether I actually like you.*

Now I don't want you to entertain such thoughts. I am above human pettiness. I am not one of those "gods" of Mount Olympus in Ancient Greece, that pathetic menagerie who *were* made in your image, and were therefore subject to all the quirks and foibles of the human heart.

But back to your statement, that *you simply don't like me*. Why don't you like me? Have you come to this conclusion on your own, or is it on the coat-tails of others, perhaps your favourite social commentator or newspaper columnist? If this is truly, honestly, your opinion and your opinion alone, then I ask one more question, *on what do you base this view?* Either it is who I am, what I have done or what I have said. If it's the very possibility of my existence that bothers you, then we have a lot to talk about.

I am guessing that, if this is the case, then you'd be a lot happier if I weren't around at all. In fact I would go further and suggest that the very idea of me rankles with you. You look at the World and perhaps say, "Look at the injustices, the hatreds, the wars. How many of them are religious in nature. What a better place the World would be if there were *no religions at all*, no gods to corrupt the heart of man and prompt him into various nastinesses".

To answer that I need to remind you of this desire for connectedness that I placed in the heart of man, when I created you in my likeness, what I call *the Longing*. It's there whether you believe in me or not. And, as I said earlier, it's when people fail to connect to me correctly and seek alternatives, even *spiritual* alternatives, that all kinds of evil can arise, leading to these injustices, hatreds and wars. You have to believe me when I say that these things tear at my heart too. You were created for good deeds, not evil deeds, but something went wrong along the way.

Mankind proclaims
We'd believe in you if we could see you.

God answers
Oxygen is invisible too, but you'd be dead without it. So is the wind but you can still feel its effects as it breezes past you. The trouble is that in your Age of Reason, anything that cannot be evaluated by your five senses is deemed to be an illusion. Your scientists tell you that anything beyond

the physical world of sight, sound, touch, smell and taste is to be avoided, disbelieved, even ridiculed. No reasons are given, no reasons are sought. It is just accepted by you, as the opinion of the experts in your Scientific Age.

A life lived solely through the senses could be a life lived selfishly, with no real regards for the World around you, unless you have made real efforts to do otherwise. It is a life without real hope too, because you are also told that what is *you* is just a unique combination of chemicals in your brain and, when that ceases to be, so do you. You may find this an acceptable state of affairs, in which case I urge you to re-evaluate, because, if my claims are true, you are rejecting the very destiny for which you were put on this Earth.

Yes, that is true, as big a thing as this is for you to understand, there is a purpose in every human life, whether that's accepted or rejected. It's always going to be *your* choice, so make it wisely.

Mankind proclaims
You have already let us down.

God answers
If this is so then I apologise on behalf of those who have *actually* let you down. Just can't get the staff, these days! The trouble is that even my own people have been known to get things wrong and some of them have messed things up in a big way! There are two fundamental errors made

here. Firstly, they may have made claims on my behalf that are simply not true and paint a completely wrong picture of me. Secondly, as my ambassadors in the World, they may have acted in ways that ought to warrant immediate recall! My followers have the potential of being both paragons or pariahs and the latter category tend to wipe out all the good that is achieved by the former.

Of course, you may still have issues with me. Perhaps you feel you've had a raw deal in life, or that you've never had an opportunity to get to know me better. Perhaps you feel that I have rejected you. These are serious concerns, but suffice to say, hold on to this one idea – I reject no-one, my door is closed to no-one, even if your life has been a mess, or if you feel you have reached irredeemable depths. Every one of you is precious to me.

Mankind proclaims
Our scientists have disproved you.

God answers
Ah, those scientists! Yes, they mean well and most are fulfilling a calling on their life but *Science* was never meant to be an alternative to me; indeed it was itself created by me as a tool to draw you back to me, to fulfil *the Longing*. Instead, many of you decided to worship the tool itself, in fact it is just a form of self-worship, revelling in your own cleverness, and intelligence. This was never my intention but it has been a consequence of a mindset that gripped

mankind over two thousand years ago and shows no sign of abating.

What has developed, particularly over the last 150 years or so, is a philosophy that has now become the default worldview for most of you in the Western World, that of *secular humanism*. Its two words paint an adequate picture of its origins and beliefs. It is secular, inasmuch as it is man-made. It is humanistic inasmuch as it is man-centred. As you can see, it has very little to do with me. It is an *alternative* to me and most of you see no wrong in this. Yet it is wrong, because you have replaced my reality with your ideas and, as you will find as your society develops, it will eventually lead you on a downward spiral to destruction.

So the scientists have not exactly disproved me as shoved me aside in their desire to redefine the World that I have created. To do this they have to account for everything that comprises my Universe. By doing so they have hit many problems and brick walls, but you are a resourceful people and they won't give up because there's too much at stake for them. One of your scientists has been honest enough to state this fact.

He said, "*We take the side of science in spite of the patent absurdity of some of its constructs, in spite of its failure to fulfill many of its extravagant promises of health and life, in spite of the tolerance of the scientific community for unsubstantiated just-so stories, because we have a prior commitment, a commitment to materialism... Moreover, that materialism is an absolute, for we cannot allow a Divine Foot in the door."* [1]

Think for yourself, my friend. You have your own mind, so use it.

Mankind proclaims
We don't like some of the bad things you have done.

God answers
This is a common position taken by many of my detractors, those who measure me by their own set of codes for life. They judge me by the morality that has developed within this secular humanistic mindset, in other words, a set of rules for behaviour in a World ruled by mankind according to its own needs and desires.

Those who know me will know that I am the great law-giver. The Ten Commandments were mine, given to mankind thousands of years ago and are, in fact, the basis for your own moral laws. I am qualified to provide these laws to you because I know you, after all I *did* make you.

But you don't know me, especially if you choose not to follow me, so how can you judge me? You don't know what motivates me just as a child fails to discern the actions of a parent, yet a child usually has an assurance that the mother and father know best and always act out of love. Just as it is

---

1   Richard Lewontin, 'Billions and billions of demons', The New York Review, 9 January 1997. p. 31.

with me. I act out of love for you, for your well-being, but the mechanism I use and the way I express myself to you may not always fall within the parameters of your understanding. You need to trust me more.

Mankind proclaims
Many terrible things have been done in your name.

God answers
Many acts may have been done in my name, by people professing to follow me, but this by no means suggests that I sanction all acts. There have been shameful crimes committed by so-called Christians and, believe me, these imposters will pay for their misdemeanours. In fact, there have been times in history when the true Church, those who have been true disciples, have had to operate on the margins or in secret because the majority of the "Christians" had followed another way, fuelled by their darkest desires rather than out of any zeal for me. Again, every single act will bear a consequence to the perpetrator. Judgement is ultimately mine.

Mankind shrugs its shoulders
Whatever.

2 *The Longing and the Winding Road*

You still may need some convincing not only that God exists but, if He does, that He's a nice guy and lines up with your expectations of Him. You may also see this whole business as a waste of time and not worth the effort, in which case I just ask you see me through this Chapter and then consider again afterwards.

You are taught the Big Bang, but have to take it on trust as no-one was around at the beginning of the beginning. You are taught the theory of evolution, but also have to take it on trust, not only that the scientists have got it right (it is, after all, just a theory – a perceived best fit of available evidence) but also that life on earth began as an 'accident of nature'. You elect politicians and political parties, trusting that they will fulfil their pledges and that they will act honourably. You also put your trust in your heroes, be they in sports, music, film or TV, expecting them to live up to their projected personae, but you don't *really* know what they get up to 'behind closed doors', until they are the subject of a media expose or investigation.

Throughout our lives we are constantly acting on trust, placing our time, money even our lives into the hands of someone else. We don't know if the taxi-driver is suicidal or about to have a heart attack, or if the pilot is drunk, or if our financial advisor isn't secretly gambling away our money. We can lessen the chance of disappointment or disaster by demanding references or medical certificates, but we still end up needing to trust another individual, probably someone we'll never see again; perhaps we're not even aware when he's performing this service for us. Life is all about trust in others, faith that they are what they say they are, and can do what they say they can do.

Yes there is a massive difference between putting our faith in flesh-and-blood and trusting an invisible, supernatural Being. This chasm in our mind has been put there by a mindset that has developed over the last few centuries, which have seen the rise of scientific rationalism matched by a corresponding drop in belief in God.

This is not something unique to us living in the 21st Century, it is simply where we currently are in history. That is an important fact. Whatever you may be told, human progress is not this journey into a scientific nirvana, with the eradication of diseases and world poverty, humungous life-spans and unlimited leisure time for all.

It isn't going to happen for a reason already given. Potentially we could improve our planet immeasurably, we could certainly deal with World poverty, but it's not our way. We mostly don't act communally, we have developed into a collection of individuals, all looking after our own and seeking to increase our share of whatever resources there are, oblivious to those who will correspondingly need to suffer a decrease in their share. It's a consequence of this secular mindset, a decrease of horizons to a safety net around all whom we love and care for, and hell to the rest!

Two hundred years ago there was a healthy regard for God. Belief was a given, an acceptable mindset. Then came *the Enlightenment* and the rise of humanism, the idea that all that we needed to create our perfect society lay between the ears of our chief thinkers. Karl Marx lay down the blueprint for a perfect fair society, not realising that human beings are incapable of implementing this, as demonstrated by the Soviet experiment. Albert Einstein and others teased out the secrets of the atom, intending peaceful purposes but again underestimating our propensity for self-destruction. Philosophers provided a myriad of solutions to the human condition, but none offered any real hope. And all this time our beliefs were eroded thanks to the unproven certainties of scientists who refused to share their World with an unseen invisible Being.

As the natural replaced the supernatural in our national psyche, the secularists and humanist opinion-formers continued to push their agenda. Christianity has been gradually marginalised, as would Islam be – if it wasn't for fear of reprisal. Freedoms to express belief in God have been battered, replaced by the secular agenda of correctness, apparent tolerance, uniformity… which all lead to one hidden agenda, *control*. Human society is never happier than when all behaviour is predictable, when all citizens are controllable.

But these movers and shakers have overlooked one thing, *the Longing*, the yearning for connectedness that lies within our hearts. With the decline in traditional faith expressions, *the Longing* finds a degree of comfort in the many alternatives thrust at us. Hence the rise of supernatural themes in popular entertainment, notably the vampire motifs in current movies and books. Superhero movies still reign, offering a form of hero worship of super-beings, not quite gods but a close fit.

Alien films are still popular, these extraterrestrial possibilities still manage to grip the heart. In a telephone poll of 1000 Americans, 60% of them believed that extraterrestrial life exists on other planets. Even some of our atheist scientists have curiously bought into this idea – that we came from outer space – to compensate for the inadequacy of the Theory of Evolution in accounting for the origin of life.

There's a laughable irony here. Millions of dollars are spent on telescopes to scan the heavens looking for signs of intelligence yet, in biology labs all over the World, microscopes see signs of intelligent design everywhere. So while they point their radio telescopes at the sky, looking for unnatural, non-random signals, in a frantic search for intelligent life, others are investigating the DNA molecule desperately trying to prove that its overwhelmingly unnatural non-randomness is no way a product of intelligence. In other words, *we have no problem with little green men, it's the Big Invisible One we can't allow for*. Or, in words already expressed, *we cannot allow a Divine Foot in the door.*

So here we are, people built with an inner itch. How we respond to this, how we scratch and satisfy its promptings, ultimately defines us. Some ignore it entirely; this state is known to the experts as *social alienation*. Reasons given are a sense of powerlessness and meaninglessness ("nothing I do matters an iota to the world around me") and normlessness ("I don't recognise the values of society anyway"). This has become more of an issue in these current days of information overload, in that society has simply become too complicated and over-connected for some people to cope with, so they retreat further into themselves. This is not a healthy state of affairs, witness the massacre at Columbine School, for instance.

For some, *the Longing* transforms into something else very different. Neglected, it feeds on itself and gives rise to unhealthiness. Addictive behaviour – whether through drugs, alcohol, sex or unusual compulsions – draws the Universe into oneself, the connections turning within and operating within an endless feedback system, which, if left unchecked, would ultimately destroy the individual from within.

Within these extremes are the usual foibles of the human heart. We yearn for connectedness. This goes beyond human relationships, our need for the touch, affection and love of another. *The Longing* is our link to the divine, an invisible cord that takes us beyond the natural and into the unspoken uncharted waters of the supernatural. We can't put our finger on it, we don't really know that it's there. Some have called it a "God-shaped" hole in our heart, with the inference that only a "God-shaped" Person (i.e. God Himself) could fill it adequately. The only one that *fits the slipper*!

Other "gods" or "enlightened ones" – whether Allah, Buddha or any from the New Age pantheon – can purloin the spiritual pathways, but will lead to *other* places. Man-made philosophies and lifestyles would lead absolutely nowhere, as all have ultimately failed in creating a workable solution for a fair society. Even some expressions of Christianity could seem a good fit, but fall short. *The Longing* has only one match, God Himself.

Again we return to the Big Answer to the Big Questions, to The Myth or Mystery, to the *Big Invisible One*. We have to come to the unavoidable and you have to decide where you stand on this.

It is not a matter of conviction, it is all about mindsets. Are you a free thinker or are you a product of your culture? A child of atheists would default to the comfortable family position, thanks to training – either subtle or overt – during the formative years. *Father Christmas, the Tooth Fairy, Jesus Christ, all myths, we're afraid*. A child of committed Christians would also follow the parental party-line. It's what you do when these viewpoints are challenged, that is all important.

So, is your disbelief in God an inherited opinion, or is it an informed decision or perhaps just a gut feeling? Did you come to a conclusion all by yourself? Have you disproved God, in your own mind? Is it that you struggle with a concept of putting your trust in that which can't be seen, heard, touched, smelled or tasted? Be still for a moment and consider these things.

It is actually quite straightforward. The onus is with God... *if He exists*.

If He's so big and powerful and all-knowing then surely He's capable of revealing Himself to those who are open-minded enough to acknowledge Him?

That's actually how He wants it, but He does want it on an even playing field. He just wants to be given a chance... (*if He exists*). He really does want to reveal Himself to you. He needs you to have eyes and ears and a mind that are open, otherwise there's no chance of you even noticing Him if He's standing right in front of you.

Now make a huge leap. Is it too much to explore the possibility of a benign God, living beyond our senses and beyond our conditioned hearts and minds? What harm could there be, just for the duration of this book, in the quietness of your heart, to think what may have been for you up to this point... unthinkable?

Our society has mostly lost its belief in God and, far worse, has lost its fear of Him. The latter is worse because unbelief is just lack of knowledge and direction, but irreverence is showing contempt and total lack of respect to one who deserves to be treated far, far better. Think about it. It is better to have no belief at all than to believe that the God who created the Universe is happy with us knowingly insulting Him, demeaning Him and relegating Him to a 'bit part' in TV sitcoms, sarcastic news editorials and (the saddest of all) those money-hungry TV preachers. Of course, there are those denizens of spirituality, the insurance agencies, who just use Him as an excuse, an *Act of God*, to avoid paying out on those instances, such as earthquakes and ball lightning for which they don't have equations.

Where do you fit in? The chances are that you have been brought up with absolutely no concept of God, particularly if you are in your thirties or younger. Being a member of a (slightly) older generation, my primary school had a compulsory assembly at the start of the day, where we recited the Lord's Prayer and we said 'grace' at lunchtime. Secondary school had Religious Education classes where *religion* meant Christianity. Also many kids were shipped off to Sunday School to give the old folk a lie in, which gave many a reluctant soul a good grounding in things of God. Not so the Thatcher generation, or Generation X, Y or Z.

Prayers have been phased out so as not to offend. Religion has become *comparative* and pesky kids are more likely to be locked in their bedrooms with an XBox on Sunday mornings.

A lot has been lost. A whole layer of human experience has been stripped away, through ignorance, not through deliberate action but because our society has moved on, away from the spiritual and towards a pleasure-seeking existence that has no time for anything that gets in the way. Holidays are seen as our right, our reward for "toiling away" a third of our daily lives, a million miles away from their original purpose, *holy*-days, days put aside to contemplate the divine.

Weekends are our new holy times for excess and indulgence, rather than Sabbath days of rest. *Because I'm worth it*, is the mantra of our day.

This seems like a bit of a rant, but it's not personal. It's an indictment of our society, not a criticism of individuals. Whether we believe it or not, freedom has been taken away from us. We are slaves to fashion and whatever the media want us to believe in or react to. And the more we allow ourselves to get sucked into popular culture, the harder it is to break free and exercise true freedoms and the harder it is to listen to God.

God is speaking to us, all the time. He speaks through nature, through design, through our conscience, through other people, through circumstances, through our reason (despite what they tell you) and through World events. We don't listen because we've forgotten how to listen, to satisfy *the Longing*. We're not sure how to tune in and our aerial has got all bent! We're not picking up His signals, but it doesn't mean He isn't transmitting them. There was no point learning to transmit radio signals if someone hadn't come along to invent radio receivers to pick them up.

Surely there's only so much the Creator of the Universe can take. He is hated to curious extremes by atheists who deny His existence, yet rarely defended adequately by those who profess to follow Him. He thinks to Himself, *if they only knew the full story, from My perspective, perhaps then they would shift their perspective away from themselves.*

And so here is His Story. And the rest is... history.

3 *What's the Story, Divine Glory?*

There are so many crazy movie plot lines around these days, especially now we have super-sophisticated special effects that enable the weirdest scenarios to seem normal. In our cinematic experience we think nothing of having aliens, whether cuddly or homicidal, living among us or we can see New York/Los Angeles/some unnamed foreign city being flattened by some epic disaster. What a generation ago was portrayed by optical illusion, papier mache monsters or hidden strings is now so lifelike that our brains are fooled, at least for 90 minutes or so, into accepting that we are watching a believable version of reality.

But in actual fact, of course, it is all an illusion, a product of fertile imaginations and highly paid pixel manipulators and our reaction to 9/11 shows how we deal with any major event that falls outside acceptable parameters – we panic and lash out. We are conservative by nature and make firm distinctions between fantasy and reality, because that is the way we are. We have created a nice safe, predictable, logical world for ourselves and woe betide any terrorist or foreign despot who tries to disrupt it.

Well, hang onto your hats, because there is a plot line that has been unfolding for thousands of years, way beyond the wildest spark of genius within the fertile imagination of a Steven Spielberg or J.J. Abrams. This plot is truly out of this World – *truly*. It is a story instigated, written, produced and directed by the master of all plot lines, God Himself. You may find this hard to swallow, but I urge you to persevere with it anyway.

It all started in a far off place called *nowhere* at a far off time called *notime*. Space and time did not yet exist, not because the Big Bang hadn't happened yet, but because God, a living intelligence – the *only* living intelligence, in fact the *only* entity in existence – hadn't yet decided to act.

This was not the beginning, because there was *no* beginning, as the clock of time hadn't yet been primed. This could have been a long wait, perhaps an infinite wait – whatever that means – we have no way of knowing. But the wait was over. God acted.

He acted. It must have been some effort, or perhaps it was just a whim (though I doubt it), but in the very first moment of our Universe, the clock started, swiftly sweeping these moments into history, an inexorable, relentless process, churning out billions of moments, leading up to you sitting comfortably reading these words, wondering where we're going to go next.

Where God went next has been the most hotly debated scientific topic of modern times, even among those who are feeding their understanding with the same words, the first few words in the Bible. And this is where the omelette hits the fan, because your understanding will be a product of your worldview, so just hold back and bear with me if we go along purely with the story *as it has been written*.

I am not pussyfooting around and will ignore the incandescent wrath of many scientists, whether Christian or otherwise. Remember, this is His Story, as He had it written, in His word to mankind. More on this later but, suffice to say, you would surely have more respect for a Christian – whether or not you agree with him – if he actually believed the words of his own Holy Book. So this is what happened next in God's autobiography.

It could have been like a whisper in the cool, still breeze or a shout, like the roar of Aslan. I'm fairly sure it wasn't the Big Bang of the scientists, the random inexplicable event. It was the voice of God and it kick-started the Universe. God spoke and time popped into existence and He called it the *Beginning*. Then God breathed in and created some room and called it the *Heavens*. In the first moment of God's creative act, He created the Heavens and the Earth, in that order. That's all there was. No Jupiter, Saturn, Betelgeuse or Black Holes. Just the Big Old Universe and tiny little Earth. He is God and He had a plan and Earth was (and is) very much a key part of this plan. That's what the words say at face value. You may disagree (as indeed do some Christians).

Are you mad, this makes no logical sense, it flies against decades of scientific research and discovery?!

As we will discover, there is much in this unfolding plot that runs counter to the wisdom of man. That is its uniqueness and any attempt to compromise on this plot serves only to diminish its Author. Analysis of the Bible, using scientific logic and understanding seems relevant, but is it? Should we be pulling this particular book apart in such a way? On the other hand, analysis of the Bible using the wisdom that comes from faith also seems relevant. It's a matter of genre. It's also a clash of worldviews. There's a lot more here than meets the eye.

There's a real battle going on here and you only tend to hear one side of it. I have simply chosen the side I wish to follow and exercise my faith accordingly. More about *the F word* later on, it's enough to say that it is a key concept.

So we have an unfilled Universe and Earth hanging there empty and alone (according to my understanding). Then God set to work, except it wasn't God as we know Him to be, it was an *aspect* of God who did the work, the aspect who interacts physically with our World and who was eventually to visit it. We will get to know this person as *Jesus*. More about him later.

Eh? What's that all about? It's in the Bible, it's actually the opening statement in the Gospel of John, but you rarely get to hear it explained in this way. So you've met the worker, what about the work? On Day One came light and darkness, day and night. On Day Two came the sky, followed by the land, seas and vegetation on Day Three. On Day Four He got round to the rest of the universe; the stars and planets and, in particular the Sun and the Moon.

A pause for thought. Scientifically it may all sound ridiculous, but if you were God and you really had these powers then wouldn't you concentrate your efforts just on one small part of your creation? Just hang onto this idea, that will be developed through this Chapter, that if the Earth – and all that lives there – is really so important, then it would be created first and the rest of the heavenly bodies would only be important as far as they are important from Earth's perspective i.e. the stars to mark seasons and the passage of time, the Sun to provide light and the Moon to control the tides. What's Alpha Centauri ever done for the Earth, after all? This is heavy stuff and, to be honest, many Christians would take the scientific line on this, but it is not something on which we should fall out with each other.

Day Five filled the seas and sky with fishes and birds, then Day Six did the same for the land with a huge variety of animals, all created fully formed in an instant.

How are we doing so far? How does it sound to you, a little bit far-out, perhaps it is nonsense to your eyes and ears? You have been brought up believing these stories as myths, even fairy-stories. But we are going to think for ourselves and one thing we must consider is how our inherited mindset governs our thinking on this story. The *Biblical* mindset is the state of mind that accepts that not only does God exist but that He has provided us with a book, The Bible, that tells the whole story from His perspective. From this I arrive at my first foundational statement.

If God exists, then perhaps we should try to understand the World from His perspective rather than judging Him from the World's perspective.

If the Earth was central to God's plans it was for one reason and one reason alone. It was because of what He created towards the end of the Sixth Day. If the first five and a bit Days were all about Earth then the rest of World history from that Day onwards is all about you and me, human beings, men and women.

We were created in God's image, something that raises us way above the rest of the animal kingdom, to the consternation of evolutionists and yourself (probably). We have been given a soul and a spirit, again at odds with evolutionists, who see us all purely as physical structures and could in no way accept a part of you that can't be classified chemically.

This is how I see it…

Adam and Eve lived in the Garden of Eden, a real place near the conjunction of three rivers in modern day Iraq. In this garden were two very special trees, the *Tree of Life* and the *Tree of Knowledge of Good and Evil*. And it's because of this latter tree that you and I are not living idyllic pain-free lives in the Garden of Eden in full communion with God and His creation. Here is the story in a nutshell.

God told them not to eat from *that* tree on pain of (spiritual) death but Eve listened to the crafty serpent who said that it was OK to do so. Eve ate the fruit, as did Adam. This was the first *sin* and, as a result, they died spiritually, gained dangerous wisdom and were banished from the Garden, sentenced to a life of pain and hardship.

Sin. What a curious word. What images does it conjure up in your mind? It has been used in an advertising campaign to sell ice cream. It's a weak, flippant word these days, most often used in the weight-loss industry for food that piles on the calories. It's a word that has been devalued like no other, like a majestic lion wrenched out of the wild and tamed in a suburban zoo. It was originally a word of weight and portent, endued with awesomeness, with power over life and death. It is now an empty shell of a word, stripped of its vitality and diluted to render it powerless.

Well that's the theory. The truth is that, while our use of the word has rendered it powerless, the meaning and implication of the word is just as strong as it has always been. It's just as relevant to us now as it has always been, it's just that we don't know it. Instead, we just ridicule it and hope that it will just go away. *Sin? Don't make me laugh, this is the 21st Century and anything goes!*

There's no such thing as 'living in sin' any more, we're all doing it! There's no harm in stretching the rules a little bit, who really cares anyway?

It's sin that causes our separation from God and we're not talking of excess calories. Perhaps better words for it these days are *misdeed* or *offence*. What we call it is immaterial; what it represents is critical. We are all separated from God by our sin and it makes no difference whether we are mass murderers or paperclip stealers, *a miss is as good as a mile.*

And this is all down to Adam and Eve! Mysteriously, ever since they ate from that fruit this sinful nature has henceforth been inherited by every person who has subsequently lived and even the very ground was cursed. This sorry state of affairs has been known as *the Fall* and is the source of just about everything that is wrong with our world, including us.

Again the rationalists (and you?) scream with indignation, *surely you are kidding, not only did Adam and Eve not exist but how can their actions affect all who have come after them?* And again I say, let's look at the whole episode from God's perspective.

God created man for a purpose. What was this purpose? Was it a social experiment to see how long it would take for humans to mess up their World? Was He lonely and bored and wanted something to do? Or is it just a part of His nature, His desire to have an object of His love. This is the acceptable answer. Believe it or not, we were all created because God loves us. *Well, He's got a funny way of showing it, with all the bad stuff in this World.* It may seem that way, but then we do need to see the full picture.

Adam walked with God in the cool of the day. He had a perfect connection with his Creator, a face-to-face relationship no less. Then came *The Fall* and all was marred, this connection was taken away and, in its place came *the Longing*.

There's a fundamental difference between Man and God and if you search your heart you will find it. We're basically not very nice. Left alone and unrestrained by society's laws, we generally become wickedly selfish and roam around looking after our needs, at the expense of others. Again, this has been a consequence of The Fall, when Adam blew it big time!

We now have to make a decision. If we are willing to believe in God and will give Him the benefit of the doubt over all that He did in that first Week of Creation, then we also have to decide if He is good – a God of Love – or evil. If He is evil, then He has lied to us over everything, the Bible is just one big deception and there's absolutely no hope for us. We're all off to Hell in a handbasket.

I for one am not willing to accept that possibility, so there's only one alternative and that is God is who He says He is. And if that is so, if He is truly a God of Love, then He really isn't like us. We may have been originally created in His likeness, but we have veered away from the template.

So there's God… and there's us. Because of that first sin of Adam and Eve and every subsequent sin that has ever been committed, there's no way we can walk with God as Adam did, "in the cool of the day". But every fibre of our being, whether we know it or not, wants to do so. That's *the Longing*.

If God truly loves us, then He's surely going to provide a way to satisfy this *Longing*. Which brings us to my second foundational statement.

From God's perspective He must be really browned off with us, but because He loves us, surely He can find a way to make things right.

So where does the plot take us next? Is there really a way back for us?

4 *Get Back... To Where You Ought'a Be!*

Yes, yes, you probably know what's coming next. Jesus stands behind the curtain, stage left, waiting for his cue. But we wait, because there are a few more plot developments first.

So here are Adam and Eve, thrown out of the garden, doomed to live their long lives in toil and sweat and creating a huge dynasty... the human race. As generation follows generation, there's a growth of goodness in some but there's mostly wickedness. *The Longing* is hijacked by man's greed, lust for power and just plain lust. God is dismayed by what He sees and thinks to Himself:

> *How great man's wickedness has become,*
> *and all that he thinks about is evil. Why on*
> *earth did I bother? Enough is enough, there's*
> *a whole lot of smiting to be done...*

God was ready to destroy all of life and would have done if it weren't for one man, Noah. Instead He sent a flood and started again with Noah, his family and the animals rescued in the ark.

Now we could argue the toss about this Flood business and look for scientific evidence for and against whether the Flood was global, regional or delusional. But, as with Adam and Eve etc., you believe what you want to believe in. It's a question of faith, the *F* word, the key that unlocks the "God Delusion". All will be explained… very soon.

Adam's dynasty had been pruned, but Noah's was going to populate the Earth and his great great great great great great great great grandson was going to usher in a whole new deal. This was Abraham, Father Abraham, who set a unique example to all who came after him, including you and me. He has been called the *Father of faith*.

Faith is the key to everything. Without it this book would never have been written and *the Longing* would have no way to be satisfied. The first stage in doing so is to acknowledge that there is a loving God who we want to connect to and *faith* is the mechanism for this great leap into the unknown, guaranteed to bring ridicule from your peer group and counter to the *zeitgeist* of modern society.

Abraham particularly showed this faith in two episodes in his life. Firstly, he left his comfortable home for a schlep across the desert to places unknown and secondly, he was willing to kill his much-loved son, Isaac, at God's command. You see, Isaac was needed as a burnt offering, to please God.

To please God? A burnt offering? Have we skipped a few chapters to "God: The Angry Years"? Are we on the same page? Yes… and this is where it gets difficult. God, what *are* You up to here?

Alfred Hitchcock and others popularised the use of the *MacGuffin* in their films, a plot device that helps to move the story along. One example would be the rosebud in Citizen Kane. Now meet the greatest MacGuffin of them all, in the Greatest (True) Story Ever Told. It's the *blood sacrifice*.

First about blood itself. Blood has great physical properties; it is vital to the movement of chemicals around the human body. But it also has other properties; it is very important to God. Why this should be… well, only God knows!

Here's what I believe…

God has given us life. He could have chosen not to. He could have decided to spend the rest of infinity alone, or He could have decided to make cats or cockroaches the objects of His love. But no, He made us, He created an ideal environment for us and mechanisms to ensure a fruitful life. But He also created rules for us to live by, particularly now that The Fall had occurred and all kinds of evil was emanating from the hearts of man and woman, prompting all kinds of acts of selfishness and nastiness.

There's a problem, but we don't know it. We think that all is well, because we are not informed otherwise. We go through life bombarded by positive messages of the nobility of the human spirit. We speak of *humanity* in teary-eyed whispers and those who fall short are called *inhuman* and accused of acting like beasts. The implication is of the basic goodness of the human race.

If we believe that we humans are thoroughly nice chaps then we must honestly ask ourselves what comes most naturally to us – good behaviour or bad behaviour. Then we must consider the following:

Why do atrocities come so naturally to conquering armies, irrespective of their nationality? Why is pornography the biggest money-spinner on the internet? Why do we need locks and security cameras? Why are our prisons bursting at the seams? Why are more policemen these days carrying firearms?

If you feel this list has been biased, just highlighting the foibles of the criminal classes of society, then how about the following?

Why are the biggest selling computer games the ones featuring acts of violence? (One of the top selling games in the past few years is *Grand Theft Auto*, a game where you can score points by chainsawing pedestrians) Why does the threshold of taste in film releases get pushed back further and further? Why are divorce rates growing and marriage rates dropping? Why are footballers better rewarded than heart surgeons? How many lottery winners give most of their winnings away to charity?

Need I go on? The fact is that we are more naturally drawn to the seamier underbelly of human existence. Acts of pure selflessness are becoming rarer these days and pure goodness is in short supply in a society where "dog eats dog" and "greed is good".

Kids are naturally naughty, it's something that doesn't need to be taught! Good behaviour *does* need to be taught. When we become adults many of us retain some of this naughtiness, even if it's just stealing pens from work, inching past the speed limit on the odd occasion or overindulging on one of the milder vices.

Ever since Adam and Eve disobeyed God and created a breach between man and God, the Bible gives us stories of our bad behaviour; Cain murdering his brother Abel, licentiousness, unnatural acts with demons, covering the whole range of bad behaviour of which we have always been capable.

Look at yourself objectively. Do you honestly believe that you have anything in common with and can stand in the presence of the One who is completely good and incapable of evil, God Himself? Well, we can't, not without special measures taken.

Think about how society governs us. There are special measures taken for every misdemeanour we may commit. Speeding in a car will result in penalty points, which could involve the confiscation of your licence. Stealing money can result in a fine. Murder will involve a lengthy stay in prison. Then there are the special measures taken in our personal relationships. Adultery could involve family breakup. Violence to others could involve retaliation. Stealing from a friend could mean the loss of that friend. There are always consequences to our misdeeds, or sins.

And this brings us back to the blood. Human logic just can't grasp it but, for God, the special measures needed for *every* sin that we commit, whether it is against society, family and friends or even the odd nasty thought, *involves the shedding of blood*.

Instead of paying a fine, going to prison, the loss of privileges, or the destruction of relationships, God expects just one act to be performed. *Something needs to be killed.* Politically incorrect or what – pass that one by the animal liberationists! It's to do with the blood and it just happens to be the mechanism that God has put in place for dealing with us and ensuring that there at least is some chance of us pleasing Him.

And that's the MacGuffin, the shedding of blood – usually a goat or a lamb – the burnt offering. And that is why Abraham has been lionised as this great man of faith, because He didn't question the fact that he was asked to sacrifice his beloved son, Isaac, instead of a goat or a lamb. He had such faith in the love and goodness and promises (of a vast dynasty) of God that he was certain that Isaac would rise again from the dead. But he would still need to slit his son's throat first.

Just remember, these were more violent and uncompromising times then, compared to our existences, insulated from the realities of our brutal World. By the way – God was just testing Abraham, Isaac lived happily ever after to a ripe old age!

Under our critical gaze it doesn't look good, this blood-thirstiness, but we must take two things into consideration here. Firstly, to God, mankind is the pinnacle of creation, the animal kingdom is there to serve us. After all, we eat enough of it without conscience, so who are we to judge God on this issue?

Secondly, is to repeat the statement – who are we to judge God on this issue? All God was saying to these first followers is that they had to perform a ritual to earn His favour and this ritual involved the death of an animal. God does not need this per se, he doesn't enjoy the smell of burning flesh, nor the sight of spilt blood. What He was asking for was the *act* of sacrifice, the willingness of mankind to take Him seriously, obey Him and seek His approval. He really would have preferred an inner attitude of heart, rather than this external action, but He had to start somewhere. This was the system He put in place for mankind to commune with Him, to help bridge the yawning chasm between man and God and we either like it or lump it.

God didn't mess about in those days and now it gets really difficult for some Christians, who would rather sweep what I'm about to say under the carpet. The fact is that God has been seen to act in very... ungodly ways in the Bible. That's us looking back and judging Him, but God the Judge was (and is) not someone you should cross in a hurry.

After all He wiped out just about everything (apart from one family, some selected animals and a load of fish) in the Flood. He demolished the evil twin towns of Sodom and Gomorrah (apart from one family). Then there was the killing of the Egyptian first-borns in the story of Moses and the Exodus, the "ethnic cleansing" of some pagan tribes and that's all in just the first few Books of the Bible.

So what picture do we have of God? Not a good one, perhaps... from our perspective. But who are we to judge? We, who routinely murder millions of unborn human beings every year, just because their lives would be an inconvenience. Abortion has its reasons, however morally unacceptable they may be. God has reasons for His actions too and we need to have enough faith to accept that they are always the *right* reasons.

So what about God's perspective? Why so much killing? Millions of innocent animals slaughtered to cover the sins of those people in the Bible. Thousands of Bible folk slaughtered because they didn't measure up. This just doesn't seem logical, necessary, or consistent with our image of a loving God who, as He tells us, considers every one of us so valuable to Him that He has even numbered the hairs on our head.

It's the great paradox because it can't be satisfactorily answered by human logic. All we can say is that *God chooses to do what He chooses*. Seemingly He cared nothing for all of those sacrificed animals yet, let's face it, neither do we, those of us who enjoy our roast lamb and beef burgers. It's sadly a feature of our World that animals generally need to die so that we may live healthily. So our moral outrage on this count is largely misplaced (apologies to you vegetarians).

Then there's the matter of those people in the Bible who were slaughtered, many of them innocent children. Some of them were destroyed directly through God's actions, others by His command, in military situations. When Joshua fought the battle of Jericho (as in the song), he was instructed to slaughter men, women, young and old, even cattle, sheep and donkeys.

To this we may as well add the cries of our own hearts, closer to home. Why do so many people die in natural disasters – there are even stories of those seeking refuge in churches during earthquakes, but still dying? Why do kids get cancer? Why are there so many nasty diseases? Why do good people (even Christians) so often die young? Why do so many evil people live to a ripe old age?

If God is in charge and if He counts every hair on our head, then surely He is answerable to these valid questions? He surely will answer them, but not to any Earthly court, neither to you and me indignantly sitting here, but to those of us given the immense privilege of one future time walking with Him in the cool of the day. Then we will know everything and will understand everything.

Bad answer, we want to know now!

That's our problem. It's all a part of something I have mentioned earlier, the mindset of people living in the developed World of the 21st Century. We want answers, we *demand* answers, to everything. We don't like uncertainties, mysteries and will always look for answers in the realm of the physical, of what we can touch, see, smell, hear and taste, because that is the scientific nature of this mindset. For those of you thoroughly immersed in this worldview, this Chapter (indeed, this book), has grated, has made you angry, has gone against everything you stand for.

Yet you are still here. Please hang around.

God is patient, God is kind. God is loving, God is generous. These are all the attributes you hear in Christmas carols and popular hymns. This is the fluffy stuff, the life of meaning and significance offered, the assurance of His love and care, the promise of life after death. Some people get the impression that this is the sum total of God's character, that this is all that there is. It's certainly a nice package, but it's not the *full* package on offer.

There are two sides to God. Think of Him as an ever-spinning coin, two sides spinning so fast that they seem as one. On the one side is patience, love and kindness and all the other virtues. On the other we see what Christians call *righteousness*, a real mouthful of a word, a meaty word that means absolutely nothing to the average person. It's an interesting word inasmuch as it can only be applied to God Himself; He is the only person in the Universe who can be called "righteous". If we understand what being *righteous* is all about, then we can get closer to the *real* person behind the ethereal mask.

Simply, it means that God is the only person who is always right. Not the 'if it's right for you'-type of *right*. We are talking about absolute rightness, as cemented into the fabric of the Universe. If there is any vagueness or indistinctness to this *right*, then the Universe would just collapse around us. It's set in stone, quite literally, when we read later that the rules He gave us to live by were actually carved by His finger on stone tablets.

So He's always right is He? I can hear you say, perhaps with a touch of cynicism. The answer to that is a firm *yes*, with the added comment that, if we accept that He created us and sustains us, then He has every right to be always… right. It means not a jot whether we accept that fact or not, it just is. Most of us live our lives in complete ignorance or in complete defiance of this fact but, the truth is, we will, one day, be held accountable for this. Which brings me to the implication of God's righteousness and that is the more familiar term of *justice*.

Justice is the principle whereby God shows us the acceptable standards of right and wrong. It also outlines the penalties that we deserve if we fall short of these standards. Without justice in society we have anarchy with *the survival of the fittest* holding sway and the law-abiding citizen a pure fantasy, as there would be no laws to abide by. A system of justice is essential to civilised society and, believe it or not, the basic principles were set in stone a few thousand years ago by God Himself.

So God has provided us with justice, a way that we can live our lives without going around killing each other willy-nilly. He also provided us with the ultimate deterrent, to make sure that we abide by the rules of this justice. Unfortunately, its impact has declined the further away our society has gone from God, but the reality of it is unchanged. The ultimate deterrent at the heart of the system of justice is fear, the *fear of God*. It's just another expression of His fatherhood. A good father always knows how to discipline his children and it's fear of this discipline that helps to moderate the behaviour of the child.

A wise man once told me that whatever you fear the most becomes your god. Be it fear of terrorism, of cancer, of boredom or of your mother-in-law, if it grips you, then you're a slave to it. It has become your god. But it's really a waste of time because it has neither the substance to acknowledge you nor the power to console you. This god is an unworthy god yet the one God that you should have a healthy fear of goes unnoticed.

We all need a healthy fear of God, because, at the very least, it acknowledges His existence. But, more importantly, it reminds us that we are dealing with a multi-dimensional being who, while burdened with the job of sustaining the known Universe, still finds time to deal with each of us individually.

His earliest followers tended to fear God more than they loved Him. That suited Him as He was moulding them as a people and a healthy fear of Him was a necessary part of this process. Although His love for them was apparent, in His nurturing of them and guiding them through perilous times, it wasn't until the time of King David, who wrote the Psalms when he wasn't slaying the baddies and laying the ladies, that we read explicitly of this love being reciprocated.

The early Christians loved and feared Him in equal measure. Fully aware of the awesome gift that had been granted to them, they benefited by a real relationship with God, grounded in love that flowed both ways. But they were ever mindful that they were dealing with the Creator God of the Universe, so there was a reverence for Him that manifested itself in healthy fear. They knew that this fear gave them wisdom and an understanding of His ways, so they accepted it as part of the package.

Unfortunately, where we are now, much (but not all) of the fear of God has been lost, to the extent that He is now rather taken for granted. Christians used to be known as "god fearing", but not so much now. We hear so much of *God is love*, as if that's all He's about. It's not that He isn't, it is just that there is much *more* to Him than that. If God is *just* about "love", then we find it very hard to answer the old chestnuts; *if God is loving then...why is there so much pain in the world? Why are there so many horrific diseases? Why do so many die from natural disasters?*

If God is just about love then these questions are impossible to answer. There must be more to Him than that, so that we are able to answer these difficult questions. Although we can never have *all* the answers, an understanding of the flip side, of the *righteousness* of God, will unlock some understanding. Perhaps we should be asking the question, *If God is so righteous then... why does He bother with us at all?*

There is one basic principle when it comes to God, one that overrules all others and one that I have already mentioned.

God chooses to do what He chooses. That's the bottom line. But it's not always the full picture. Our own individual free-will is also part of the picture.

There is an element of cause and effect. In Bible times, God's people were always given a choice, to follow Him or *not* follow Him. If they followed Him, they were given success in battle, prosperity, peace, safety and a full womb. If they turned their back on Him (and many, unbelievably did), then none of these blessings was guaranteed, only curses. *Choose life*, He said, but, as is the way of mankind at all points of history, we just like to do things *our way*.

Our way? Frank Sinatra spoke for all of us here ("I did it... My Way"). We follow our own plans, we create our own plot lines, not realising that every one of us is part of a Greater Drama. It is now summarised in a nutshell.

> *Here He is, the Creator of everything in the
> Universe, from the amoeba to the supernova.
> He decides that, out of all Creation, only the
> human race is going to experience fellowship
> with Him. Not all are going to want to do
> so, but He wants to give all a chance, so He
> unfolds a plan. He allots every human being
> a time span on Earth, unique in length and
> circumstance, and, in ways known only to
> Him, gives everyone a chance to receive
> Him or reject Him. Those who receive Him
> are granted fellowship with Him forever,*

allowed to avoid the inescapable and awful consequence of rejecting His love, a nasty place called Hell.

Now, how exactly does this work... ?

5 *Here Comes the Son*

||||||||||||||||||||||||||||||||||||||||||||||||||||||||||||||||||||||||||||||||||||||||||||||||||||||||||||||

The central character is about to make his appearance. He still stands behind the curtain and he is about to take his cue.

He has been waiting a long time, since the Creation of the World, the Universe and everything, in fact. He is about to return as the *main act*.

Before he does we set the scene.

God's people in the first half of the Bible were the Israelites, the descendants of Abraham. They were the main players, through whom God worked in the Bible lands. It was their armies who conquered the land at God's bidding. It was their prophets who proclaimed blessings or woes, and it was their sins and disobedience that brought them exile, first to Assyria, then Babylon, though they also sustained a continued presence in the land now known as Israel.

God is saddened at how stupid and stubborn human beings are. These Israelites just had to choose life and they would have had it all, but instead they went their own way. The end result was, for the great majority, exile from their land. For the rest, a life of hardship as a subjugated people, living under harsh Roman rule around two thousand years ago.

Then God said to Himself, *it is time. Now, son, go and do your stuff.*

It's a fact that over-familiarity can provoke indifference, even impatience, but if we were ever able to grasp the basic awesomeness of what *did* happen next, everything else in our mind would be swept away immediately. It is something that we could never fully grasp, because it is far beyond our capabilities to do so.

This is what happened.

As already explained, God had created His plot-device, the shedding of innocent blood, as the only way for man and God to be reconciled. This system had been implemented through animal sacrifice, at the Temple in Jerusalem for hundreds and hundreds of years. It wasn't a perfect system. In fact it was a logistical nightmare, bearing in mind the number of people around and the number of sins being committed. Of course, if this were still around now, with people and sins running into billions, our rivers would literally be flowing with animal blood.

So, what are the implications? If the shedding of blood is the only way for us to be right with God, and being right with God is the only way in life to be really blessed, then why aren't we still doing it?

Because God provided *another* way. He, Himself, the Creator of everything, dropped out of eternity, to live as a human being in His Creation. It wasn't a social visit, a royal state visit to meet and greet the people. It wasn't a landlord's fact-finding tour, to ascertain whether all was hunky dory and whether there was scope for improvements. It wasn't a PR campaign, He wasn't a "secret millionaire", to endow riches on some unsuspecting individual.

No, it was the ultimate and undeniable expression of His love for His creation. This wasn't a sentimental, distant or safe love from afar. This was a love that crossed the greatest boundary of all to express itself. It was a love that took God from the unimaginable majesty of Heaven to be born in the dirt of a cave to an unmarried peasant girl in an insignificant city in an occupied land. No-one could dream up such a contrast, it was the ultimate fall in personal circumstances. That's how much God loves us and that was just the start of it.

Jesus grew up in a poor home and, when he wasn't helping his stepdad in the workshop, was gaining in knowledge of Holy Scriptures, as was the norm for Jewish boys at that time. He lived an average life until his early thirties when he began the mission that he put himself on Earth for.

In a period of just over three years he dedicated his life to the people who surrounded him, from his twelve close friends, to his wider following and ultimately to the whole Jewish nation. He wandered around endlessly, teaching, preaching, healing, performing great miracles, from walking on water to raising the dead. He was approachable to people from all walks of life, even women and children, though he had stern words for religious hypocrites. At all times he kept up his connection to the

Divine and prayed often and lengthily to God (this is not the time to discuss the apparent paradox of God praying to himself). He was also the only sinless man ever to walk the Earth.

In that same period he put up with rejection (even from those close to him), betrayal, abuse, lies and misunderstandings, lack of appreciation, threatened violence and endless arguments with the religious authorities. But this was nothing compared to what was thrown at him on his last day on Earth.

He was arrested. After a sham trial the Jews spat at him, mocked him, struck him and slapped him. Then the Romans flogged him until the flesh on his back was shredded, then lacerated his head with a crown made out of the nastiest thorns, mocked him, spat on him, then struck him on the head again and again.

Then he was crucified by the Romans, in full view of the people. Crucifixion involved nails driven through both hands and feet into a wooden stake, or cross. As he slowly sags down with more weight on the nails in the hands, the need to breathe forces him upward in excruciating pain, then he places his full weight on the nail through his feet and more unspeakable agony. Hours of unimaginable pain... but for him it was to get worse.

First we need to understand something. Jesus was fully aware that this was going to happen to him, he had seen it coming and it had also been prophesied about, hundreds of years earlier. He was also God and knew what was really happening and also knew that, as appalling as the physical pain was… it was about to get very much worse.

If you were asked why you think Jesus was sent to Earth, the usual answer would focus on the good deeds that he performed and the timeless teachings he gave. *Surely he came to teach us to live?* Well, this was true, but it wasn't the main reason. By far the most important reason for God to visit Earth in the form of Jesus… *was to die.*

And to understand this we need to return to our MacGuffin, our plot-device, the shedding of blood, the burnt offering, the sacrifice. This was, as you remember, God's mechanism to allow us to get right with God for every sin that we commit, whether it's stealing a pencil from the office or stealing the wife of the office manager. Why this should be is a complete mystery, it *just is.*

God added a corollary to this rule, a great sacrifice for Him but an unbelievable free offer to us, no strings attached. It states that, if God were to offer *Himself* as a sacrifice, then, because it's Him and not a goat or lamb, this single sacrifice would cover the sins of everyone… just like that. This is incredible and is the ultimate act of love. Again, why this should be is a complete mystery, but we should be unbelievably thankful for it, as we will find out soon in our story.

For this to happen, God would need to be born of a woman and live with us and, when the time was right, offer Himself as a perfect sacrifice. This is what He did and this is how He did it.

He had now been hanging in agony on the cross of crucifixion for three hours. Then, suddenly, in the middle of this Spring day, darkness came over the whole land for three hours. What happened in those three hours of darkness, three hours when Jesus' face was hidden from us?

This was when Jesus, *literally*, died for our sins. How many times have you heard that phrase, and yet it has probably never impacted you? This is because the words had no meaning for you. Hopefully, they do now. It was a conscious, real, physical act that Jesus went through on that cross. This means that, somehow every sin ever committed by every person who ever lived was dealt with by Jesus during those three hours of darkness.

And it explains the darkness, because it was not a pretty sight, it was not something that mortal man could or would want to behold. So God, in His mercy, provided darkness for us, not for Jesus. He still had to go through this untold agony, added to the physical agony of the crucifixion. No wonder, when it was all over, that he cried out to God, "Why have you forsaken me?" It is just too awful for us to comprehend and this is why we must be so, so grateful.

But this is only the half of the story, the *bad* half. There is a happy ending because, a couple of days later, after being buried in a tomb, guarded by Roman soldiers... he returned to life, spoke to his friends, ate some fish and then returned to Heaven.

Yes, but what does it mean? If the crucifixion provided a way for us to have *the Longing* satisfied, to get right with

God so that He can bless us, then this return from the dead, the *resurrection*, provided a way for us to defeat death.

This ought to make you really excited, if only you can exercise the faith needed to weld it to your soul. Jesus' death helps you to live a life of meaning, working out your life in partnership with God, and his resurrection promises that eventual physical death is not the end of the story, but, for those willing to embrace it, a glorious beginning.

Stuff and nonsense, or *Give me some of that*? The choice is yours. Walk away now and you may not get another chance. It will be bad enough living a life of wasted opportunities, of lost blessings, hope, fellowship and understanding. But dare you risk an uncomfortable eternity (that's an awful long time) away from the presence of the God you have rejected in this life?

Jesus may have died for you but this fact will have absolutely no relevance or power in your life unless you accept it by faith. This means that you have to accept with the core of your being that everything you have read in this book could well be true. It doesn't work by mumbling a set of half-understood formulae, mouthing disjointed Bible verses with the apparent power to impact your soul without any input from you. It requires an act of will on your part, which for some of you may be exceedingly difficult.

Perhaps you need a bit more encouragement and food for thought. Well, these are now provided, in the form of the evidence of faith-driven lives, in the next chapter.

6

Go Tell it On the Mountain

There are not many things worth dying for. You have to be either mad, super-heroic or convinced that there is more to come. Surely only a madman would die willingly for no reason. A hero would die for his country or family out of love or loyalty. But would you die for your faith unless you are absolutely certain that there is substance in this faith?

That's what most of Jesus' close friends did. His brother, James, was put to death by the King. According to historical writings, the fate of the others ranged from crucifixion (Andrew, Bartholomew, Peter, Philip), stoning (the other James), beheading (Paul) to impaling (Thomas).

All these men had to do to escape cruel execution was to deny their faith. They had to be pretty sure of what they believed, to refuse to renounce it on pain of a horrible death. All had met Jesus personally (Paul's meeting was in a vision), had probably seen him die and had seen him after his death. They were the first generation of believers, with no real testimonies but their own, so they had to be very, very sure that they really had met Jesus after his death, that they didn't imagine it or dream it up.

One certain thing was that they didn't make it up – *would you die horribly for a lie*? Their deaths are matters of historical record, so, unless they were all completely bonkers – along with the countless others of their generation who died for their faith – they must really have witnessed the resurrection of Jesus Christ. Are you willing to concede that possibility?

Just think about it. What incentive would they have had to make it up? Could they have made it all up and then died an excruciating death for absolutely no purpose? Early Christianity grew as a result of personal witness of the incredible miracles, healings and tales of transformed lives, set to a backdrop of hostility from the ruling Roman and Jewish authorities. Could it have all been a delusion? If so, this delusion had a cast of several thousands, spread over many cities and lands. A groundless faith could never have delivered the goods to an extent that people were willing to die for what they had experienced and for their future hope of eternal life.

History is awash with such tales. Under the crazy Roman emperor Nero, Christians were stitched into skins of animals and set upon by dogs or just set on fire. Yet they refused to deny their faith. The emperor Trajan put to death thousands every day. One of his victims was the Church Father, Ignatius, who cried, as he was about to be devoured by lions, "*I am the wheat of Christ: I am going to be ground with*

the teeth of wild beasts, that I may be found pure bread."
Another Christian, Germanicus, behaved with such courage
that several observers were converted on the spot, impressed
that a faith could inspire such fortitude.

A procession of such witnesses marches on through
history, even up to modern times, a full 2,000 years since
Jesus walked the Earth. Here is the story of Paul Schneider,
a German pastor who lived at the time of Hitler. He was
one of the few German church leaders who actually stood
up against the Nazi madman, which got him arrested
many times from 1934 onwards. He refused to budge and
held on to the true faith in Jesus Christ, which put him in
the minority in the German Church, most others adapting
doctrines to serve Nazi ideologies and turning a blind eye to
the growing atrocities.

He persisted in this campaign and even started
excommunicating Church members who had joined the
Nazi party. For this and other acts of conscience he was
continually arrested and eventually sent him to Buchenwald
concentration camp. Even there he provided a continual
witness to his beliefs and preached from the window of his
prison cell. Two years later he was killed by lethal injection
and his funeral attended by hundreds of brave people, all
watched by the Gestapo.

Schneider could have had an easy life, as did many of
his fellow pastors, who compromised, thus ensuring their
personal safety. But his faith held fast. He had not walked
with Jesus, or heard his teachings first hand, but two thousand

years of brave witness had convinced him that one does not compromise on the truth. Death held no fear for him because he knew beyond all doubt that it was not the end and that a glorious future lay ahead of him.

Most of us are not tested to such an extreme, but we must be ready. For those of us who have tasted God working in our lives, we know that it's not just a case of intellectually accepting the claims and answers provided by Christianity. We have not just gone to a "metaphysical market" and made our choice on the basis of logic and a good marketing campaign. We are not just trying it out to see if it fits our particular needs. No, it's more like God is trying us out to see if we've got what it takes.

You see, being a Christian, a follower of Jesus Christ, is not in any way like following a philosophy or lifestyle or any of the menagerie of alternative religions there are out there. It is a full makeover, mind, body, soul and spirit, everything which is you will be overhauled, re-aligned and redirected. It is rediscovering a lost heritage, becoming the full person God always intended you to be, not the aimless, self-seeking, passion-driven automaton that society would prefer us all to become. Strong words, but, in the final analysis, that's what our secular society has forced us into. We have been homogenised, moulded into convenient templates. To the capitalist economy we are consumers, to the government we are tax reference numbers, to media moguls we are viewers or listeners. I don't want to be one of the *general public*, I want to be me and that's what God offers, a route back into our true destiny.

What a load of nonsense, Christianity is just a crutch for those who can't cope with life.

That's what bad PR gets you, together with low expectations, adverse propaganda and the terrible example set by some who profess to be Christians. It is a sad indictment that although the best advert for the Christian life can be the words and actions of Christians, so also can the worst advert be! Don't judge God by these latter folk. Our God is not a limp-wristed, out of touch peace activist, who will stand up for anything except the uncompromised, timeless and uncomfortable truth. He is not like this, neither should Christians be.

In fact it is a lot easier fleeing from God than accepting Him. The real Christian life is not for wimps. It requires, in the first instance, a complete honest appraisal of your life so far and an admittance of the many times you've really messed up. It expects you to remove yourself from the pedestal you have climbed on to and to start putting others first, even those awkward time-wasters who occupy the unwanted periphery of your daily life. It encourages you to give up those former activities that have been holding you back (however pleasurable they may seem), such as casual sex, drinking, drug taking and gambling.

Not a good advert to attract your average 21st Century hedonist, is it? Not if you're happy to continue to be one, living a life that doesn't really lead anywhere, with no legacy or purpose. I want to repeat what I said in a previous Chapter, then I will speak of my journey.

*Here He is, the Creator of everything in the
Universe, from the amoeba to the supernova.
He decides that, out of all Creation, only the
human race is going to experience fellowship
with Him. Not all are going to want to do so,
but He wants to give all a chance, so He unfolds
a plan. He allots every human being a time span
on Earth, unique in length and circumstance,
and, in ways known only to Him, gives everyone
a chance to receive Him or reject Him. Those
who receive Him are granted fellowship with
Him forever, allowed to avoid the inescapable
consequence of rejecting His love.*

We are all called, but few answer the call because we are unwilling to admit we need God and would prefer to live our lives as sole pilot, wherever that may take us.

Have you got it yet or are you still not convinced?

It took me ten years to act on the niggling growing certainties that the claims of Jesus Christ were true and unavoidable. The *Longing* had reached bursting point and all that was needed was the decision of my will to act on the knowledge I had gained and make a declaration of faith that:

◊ Although my conditioned scientific mind tells me that the ideas of virgin births, walking on water and resurrections are impossible... I am willing to believe that they are true.

◊ I admit that I have made a mess of my life and have lived it selfishly, carelessly and purposelessly... and I believe that God can put me on the right path and help me to discover the real purpose of my existence.

◊ Every fibre of my natural being is fighting against this because I am fearful what may come next and not sure if I can measure up... but I am willing to trust in God to guide me into a new life.

◊ I know that I am going to be persecuted, reviled, lampooned and ridiculed by my peers... but I am willing to put my faith above my pride.

Now, twenty five years later, I know it was the best decision I ever made. It didn't bring me a guarantee of health, wealth or success but instead it instilled in me a different set of values, a different way of looking at life, that tell me that the former things are not important. What is important now is the knowledge and absolute certainty that God is with me and will never leave me.

And it all boils down to that *F* word, faith. It's the key to it all, as I've said before. It is also the most reviled and misunderstood principle in today's world.

In the next Chapter I am going to explain why.

7 *Two Tribes Went To War*

What makes us tick? Matthew Arnold, a 19th Century English cultural commentator, thought he knew. He wrote about it is his essay, *Culture and Anarchy*.

> We show, as a nation, a great energy and
> persistence in walking according to the
> best light we have. We may regard this
> energy, this obligation of duty, self-control,
> and work as one force. And we may regard
> the intelligence driving at those ideas, the
> indomitable impulse to know and adjust them
> perfectly, as another force. And these two
> forces we may regard as in some sense rivals,
> as exhibited in man and his history and rivals
> dividing the empire of the world between
> them. And to give these forces names from
> the two races of men who have supplied
> the most signal and splendid manifestations
> of them, we may call them respectively the

forces of Hebraism and Hellenism. Hebraism and Hellenism, between these two points of influence moves our world.

He saw the British society of his day governed by these forces, Hebraism and Hellenism, which basically boils down to ideas from Ancient Israel vs. ideas from Ancient Greece. How relevant is this to us living in the developed world of the 21ˢᵗ Century? Does this still hold for us and, if so, how? To understand this we need to go back around 2,500 years.

There were two Greek philosophers who arguably have been more influential in our history than any others. One was Plato and the other Aristotle, his pupil. Plato was the more spiritually minded of the two and from his teachings came the idea of a duality of man, a separation between the body and the spirit, compartmentalising each of them. This idea seeped into areas of medicine, sociology and even into religion, where it created total havoc, particularly in the development of Christian theology and practice. More of this later.

Aristotle was more earthy in his approach and his ideas were highly influential in the early development of the scientific method. His ideas, too, crossed over into Christian theology, thanks mainly to the efforts of the Medieval theologian, Thomas Aquinas, who decided that the best way for the Church to move forwards with the times was to add human reasoning into the mix, the rationalism as developed through Aristotle's teachings working together with the faith element that came from the Jewish roots.

By the time we reach our man Matthew Arnold in the 19th Century, this historical process seems to have reached a point where the world of thought could be split into two very different forces, those of Hellenism (Greek thought) and Hebraism (Hebraic thought). He went on to say:

The uppermost idea with Hellenism is to see things as they really are; the uppermost idea with Hebraism is conduct and obedience... the Greek quarrel with the body and its desires is that they hinder right thinking, the Hebrew quarrel with them is that they hinder right acting.

So first impressions are that Greek thought is bound up in *thinking about things*, whereas Hebraic thought is all about *doing things the right way.*

He continues:

> *The governing idea of Hellenism is spontaneity of consciousness; that of Hebraism, strictness of conscience. Christianity changed nothing in this essential bent of Hebraism to set doing above knowing. Self-conquest, self-devotion, the following not our own individual will, but the will of God, obedience, is the fundamental idea of this form, also, of the discipline to which we have attached the general name of Hebraism.*

So Arnold equates Christianity, with its accent on obedience to the will of God, with Hebraism. One further quote from him to really seal the deal on this:

> *As Hellenism speaks of thinking clearly, seeing*
> *things in their essence and beauty, as a*
> *grand and precious feat for man to achieve,*
> *so Hebraism speaks of becoming conscious*
> *of sin, of awakening to a sense of sin, as a*
> *feat of this kind. It is obvious to what wide*
> *divergence these differing tendencies, actively*
> *followed, must lead.*

So, what is the point of all of this? What is this all leading to? Bear with me, because this is really going somewhere, once we grab the implications of what he is saying.

He has clearly defined what Christianity is supposed to be about. He equates it with *Hebraism*, which makes sense as the Christian faith grew from Hebraic, Jewish roots in Biblical times. This Hebraism is about following God, being aware of sin and acting on these things. So there we have, in the red corner, Hebraism, the first of the twin forces that shape our World.

And, in the blue corner, *Hellenism*, Greek thinking. This is the other force, the one that really drives the dominant worldview and mindset of our Western culture in the 21st Century. It is undergirded by the rationalist approach pioneered by Aristotle and concerns itself with thinking and analysing, thoughts rather than actions.

Christianity of old is a *revealed* religion, defined by the words of the Bible, taken in faith by Christians, but now, thanks to the infiltration of *Hellenism*, every Christian doctrine was going to be re-evaluated through the twin filters of faith and mind.

The result of this was disastrous for the Church as it was originally defined by its first leaders in the 1st Century, the Gospel writers and other Biblical writers, such as Paul, Peter and John. It meant that the goalposts would now forthwith be moved, in accordance with new thoughts and developments from the Christian thinkers of the day rather than accommodating the doctrines as originally accepted by faith from the Bible itself. As time went by, this simple idea grew and grew, with the result that Christian doctrines and practices began to be shaped more and more through what seemed logical to the mind, rather than what God seemed to be saying through His word, taken by faith. Out of this came *humanism*, placing man's intellect at the centre of everything rather than God.

Now here's the rub. Christianity today has moved on from being Hebraic, as it was in its formative years. Now it is an amalgam of the Greek and the Hebraic, thanks to the rise of rationalism and humanism and the subsequent questioning of matters of faith. And what does this result in? Let me tell you.

It produces church leaders who are turning their analytical intellects to key issues that were once taken as a matter of faith. A good example of this was David Jenkins, the once infamous (and best forgotten) Bishop of Durham, who managed to rise through the ranks of the Church of England without believing in that most crucial lynchpin of the Christian faith, the *resurrection*, calling it "a conjuring trick with a bag of bones"!

This is what happens when Greek thinking invades. It can produce confused Christians, who have difficulties with fitting their Christianity in with the World's systems and particularly with the claims of the scientists in such areas as evolution and cosmology. More about that in the next Chapter but, for now, it will be good to have a clear look at the *F* word, *faith*, as it is the cornerstone that supports the whole Christian edifice.

It's really simple. Without faith, Christianity hasn't a leg to stand on, it just becomes a philosophy. There are plenty of non-Christians who gain much benefit from the moral and ethical teachings of the Bible, without having an ounce of faith in the God of the Bible. In fact the Bible has contributed more to the moral and ethical base of our society than any other book, by a long way. Its influence is not just in religious circles but the whole of western civilisation was founded on principles laid out within its pages, on matters of law, education, language and behaviour.

The Bible itself explains what faith really is. It is being *certain of what we do not see*. It is an act of your will to accept the possibility that there is an Entity out there who you can't see (or hear, or smell, or touch or taste) but nevertheless exists and is asking you to believe in Him and trust Him. He wants you not just to believe in Him but to receive Him into your life to such an extent that a part of Him, The Holy Spirit, will reside within you and act as your guide, teacher, helper and prompter for the rest of your life.

It's a big ask, but it's surely a win-win situation. If He does exist, and does everything He promises He will do, then you are embarking on an incredible journey that will take you to some amazing places and will assure you that your life has true purpose. If He doesn't exist – and you'll have to be very sure about this – then you've lost little, just some time and perhaps a touch of pride and can live the rest of your life doing whatever you want, whatever the consequences.

But, be warned. Faith ought to be having a true expectation that something is going to happen, it's not a cynical exercise in trying to prove your Christian friends wrong. It's like that first time you let go of the side of the swimming pool and launch yourself into the water. You must *want* it to work, you must have the expectation that you're not going to sink. You're not doing it to disprove the laws of flotation through your drowned body, you're doing it because you really want to swim! Exercising faith may be an experiment, but it *must* be whole-hearted.

So here you are. You've challenged God to show His existence to you and you've assured Him that, if this were so, then you will follow Him and do all that you are meant to do, to back that up. You've made the plunge and nothing happens. What were you expecting, a heavenly choir of angels greeting you, a mighty ethereal voice welcoming you, a surge of electricity riveting you to the spot?

All these confirming signs could happen, of course, but mostly they don't. There may be a sense of assurance or there may be absolutely nothing. You are probably going to have to give it time. There's a precedent for that, after all God has waited long enough for you to make this first move. But He will move, in His own way and when you look back to those early days with the benefit of hindsight, you will marvel at how He moved in your life in the way that was uniquely just right for you.

Faith is being relentlessly eroded in our secular society as we are encouraged to seek answers in *what we see*, looking to our politicians and scientists for answers, as well as our gadgets and devices and, of course to our wallets. *Surely money can buy us anything our heart desires?* We have substituted material certainties for spiritual possibilities and it is so sad. Dare you raise your head above the parapet and act according to what your conscience may be telling you to do, even now?

So, given what God seems to be offering those who have made the decision to follow Him, you would expect people of faith to always be able to demonstrate how their lives have been enriched, to an extent that others are compelled to exclaim, *I want some of what they have!*

Yes, you would *think* that.

8 *While My Vicar Gently Weeps*

You've heard of Billy Graham, haven't you? Perhaps the most well-known Christian of the past fifty years. His shtick was to hold huge "crusades" (poor choice of words if you are a Jew or Muslim) in cities all over the World, where many thousands of people were herded into stadiums, arenas or conference centres and presented with the Christian message. Before leaving they were offered a chance to respond to the message, in the form of an agreement to a set of principles, a short prayer and a public declaration that they had now become Christians. According to his organisation, in 1993, more than 2.5 million people had been converted in this way; in one case, in Moscow, a quarter of all attendees!

Now look at it in another way. The very first Church, two thousand years ago, was founded by just twelve disciples/ apostles, who lit a flame that was to sweep through the Mediterranean lands of that day. Just twelve people! Imagine what 2.5 million people could accomplish!

Well, we're still waiting. All we can say is that times have changed and that there's a world of difference between a 1st Century citizen of Rome responding to the Christian message and a 21st Century citizen of the World doing it. The former guaranteed himself a life full of danger, uncertainty and the possibility of a martyr's death. The latter has possibly conducted a spur-of-the-moment transaction, encouraged by an emotional atmosphere, filing it away in the back of the mind as *"I'll get back to this when I have a moment, when I'm less busy"*.

If those 2.5 million people, added to all the other millions who have similarly responded to the Christian message at other meetings, by other evangelists, had truly undergone an earth-shattering, life-wrenching lasting spiritual experience then that ought to have created a hugely influential and effective army that should have transformed society at every level.

This doesn't seem to be the case. Most seem to have fallen away or just assumed that the one-time declaration was all there was to it and now they can just get on with their own lives, secure in the view that heaven is waiting for them. That's really not what it's all about but, sadly, many believe that they had just bought a lottery ticket guaranteeing a positive outcome, regardless of how they lived their lives. Did they really become Christians? Who is a Christian, after all? Truly, only God knows but the following questions need to be asked:

◊ Is the mere recitation of a set of packaged statements (called, by some, the Five Spiritual Laws) at one stage of your life sufficient to earn God's favour?

◊ Can you become a Christian as a result of being "christened" as an infant?

◊ Are you truly a Christian if you have shown no discernable change in your behaviour and outlook?

◊ All those "Christians" of yesteryear, who fought brutal "Holy Wars" *in the Name of Christ*, are they in Heaven?

I won't answer these questions, I just want to refer back to the first foundational statement I made in Chapter Three: **If God exists, then perhaps we should try to understand the World from His perspective rather than judging Him from the World's perspective.**

God means business. And He knows if we really mean business or if we're just playing at it. Becoming a Christian is not just a matter of filling out forms and making a set of declarations, it is about forming a relationship with God. The essence of a relationship is the effort put into it by *both* parties to make it work. It's an ongoing situation and is one of growth, if both parties mean business. Well, God always means business so it's up to the Christian to decide, in his heart of hearts, if his actions, thoughts and motivations are consistent with an ongoing relationship with God. Has *the Longing* been satisfied, or has it been tricked into silence?

We human beings, we love playing games. We meander around, our chests puffed out, making a lot of din, like free range chickens cheerfully oblivious of their tasty fate. We create scenarios for ourselves, where we are perfectly justified in everything we do, according to some arbitrary set of rules or standards, which are usually what is currently acceptable in society today. For example, *living in sin* is now a quaint expression and is society's norm in terms of relationships, yet just a few decades ago it was actually seen as a *sin*, frowned upon, and was the exception. Marriage between virgins was the norm then, now it is the exception.

Similarly, look and see what is acceptable in polite conversation these days. "Four letter words" (what a quaint expression) fail to shock these day, they are so commonplace, they even pepper the dialogue of our TV sitcoms. Sex and violence similarly are becoming increasingly acceptable, as media producers push against the boundaries of decent behaviour, knowing that titillation and excitement attract audiences. Each time the censor takes a step backwards, something dies inside us but we are already too deadened to realise it.

Society even encroaches upon the realms of religious life, when the World invades the spirit and the Christian can fall into the trap of confusing the two. How else do we get the usual negative Christian stereotypes? Here are some recent newspaper headlines to illustrate this:

> *Church encourages worshippers into debt so they can donate more.*

> *He's ignorant, crude and un-Christian. But don't expect the spineless Church to banish Bishop Pete.*

*'Bonking Bishop' loses dismissal claims
over affairs.*

*Faith healer quits after 'unhealthy
relationship' with female co-worker.*

It doesn't have to be this way. For every bonking Bishop we have a tireless street evangelist. For every greedy Church we have a warm, welcoming fellowship where love abounds. It's not all bad news in the Christian scene, but it could be better. Perhaps you could make a difference?

As I've said already, it's not easy being a true Christian these days, a follower of Jesus Christ who is unafraid to declare himself despite the resulting hostility and ridicule! A person who does his best to be a good witness and is humble enough to admit when he has done wrong. That's what I'm selling in this book, but it's important that you're not getting a sanitised view of things.

One thing that needs to be clear is that *becoming a Christian is about following Christ, not other Christians.* It will be your unique journey, but, at its heart will be a growing relationship between you and God, you and Jesus Christ your saviour. Other people will join you on this journey, but as fellow travellers, not as substitutes for the real thing. If that confuses you, let me explain further.

In the previous Chapter you may remember the two Greek philosophers, Aristotle and Plato. I mentioned that Plato promoted the idea of a duality of man, a separation between the body and the spirit and how this created total havoc in the development of Christian theology and practice. This is where I get to explain how.

For Plato, everything to do with the soul and spirit was good, but everything to do with the body was bad. Anything spiritual was good, anything physical was bad. Unfortunately, this idea managed to worm its way into the Christianity of the 2nd Century onwards, and did a lot of damage. It produced celibate priests, for a start, something that has cost the current Catholic Church dear in compensation pay-outs (figure that one out for yourself). How could this be? Well, the immediate effect of declaring the body as bad and soul as good is an obvious one. If the body is bad then so are things associated with the body, particularly voluntary processes like sex. To the early Church, those who followed "spiritual" careers, in the Church, were expected to be celibate, a practice that continues in the modern day Catholic Church. Monks were required to be celibate and some of them were even resistant to the idea of taking a bath, in case they saw themselves naked! A Catholic view is still that celibacy is a "higher calling", in the sense of remaining pure until heaven beckons, when you will be united with Christ directly.

But, more relevantly to us, this *duality* created two kinds of Christians, the clergy and the laity. The former were the priests, bishops and their like, the "spiritual" ones who did all the "religious" duties and the latter were the rest of us, the "physical" ones, who did what they were told. This idea, unconsciously, is still with us. The Church still has clergy, whether they are priests, bishops, vicars, ministers, prophets or whatever. The idea that there are two types of Christians is not from the Bible, which states that *all* Christians are equal and have gifts of service. It is from Plato, the Greek philosopher, that the duality comes.

The damage that this does is to create a Christian who doesn't think for himself, who slavishly (and often, lazily) follows his spiritual "leader" in matters of conduct, doctrine and theology. The trouble is, who says his leader has got it right? Thankfully, most of them have, but some Christian leaders are, sadly, little different from their secular counterpart; ambitious, persuasive and often with an agenda of their own. You can see this with some so-called "TV evangelists" and "prosperity teachers", who create their own kingdoms on Earth, funded by the gullible. Other Christian leaders are just like driftwood, but hide it well and draw folk into being as aimless and ungrounded as they are.

Not a good advert, admittedly, but I feel it necessary to warn you of the pitfalls before you embark on this amazing journey.

Follow Jesus, no-one else.

As I said, the Christian road is not an easy one, but it's the road that God has mapped out for you and, as long as your eyes are on Him, then you will not go wrong.

9 *Signed, Saved, Delivered*

It's all about good news, really. There's no down-side.

We should be shouting it from the rooftops, declaring it over every available tannoy system, broadcasting it over the airways, cramming it into every nook and cranny of the information superhighway.

Your life can make sense.

You can make an impact, whoever you are, wherever you live, whatever your circumstance, whatever bad hand you may consider you have been dealt.

And all you need is the *F* word, *faith*. Just an accepting of what you may have been told is unacceptable. Don't listen to those who have rejected this free gift, don't let them drag you down, be bold and go for it.

Hopefully, by now you have a better appreciation of the forces that drive our society, how the relentless drive towards rationalism and secular humanism has forced faith into dark corners. It's not that any discoveries have been made to discredit God, it's just the increasing need for man to be able to control his World. This can only be done by eliminating anything that can't be understood, such as the world of the supernatural. It's not just God who is denied, even belief in ghosts and the darker side of the supernatural has been in decline. Religion, magic, ghouls, unexplained phenomena, all cast into the box marked 'lunatic fringe'. God forbid that anything should distract modern man and woman from the *important* things of life... reality tv, celebrity watching and the antics of our sportsmen.

But that's enough about us. It's worth reviewing my second foundational statement from Chapter Three:

From God's perspective He must be really browned off with us, but because He loves us, surely He can find a way to make things right.

This reminds us that we are the biggest problem in our World. Left unchecked we would have destroyed the World in a myriad of ways by now. In fact, it's a wonder you're still alive to be reading this, if you think about it. If the warnings presented to us with such earnest certainty by scientists, environmentalists, astronomers, astrologers, doom-merchants, Nostra-damn-us-alls and religious nuts had come true, we'd just be a collection of atoms spread over an area previously occupied by Planet Earth. Yet we've survived despite the millennium bug, various threats of Armageddon, invasion from space, gamma ray bursts, global warming, comets from the Kuiper Belt, nuclear, chemical and bacteriological options for mass destruction, mega-tsunamis, bird and swine flu, meteors, earthquakes, AIDS, SARS, other plagues, nuclear, bacteriological and chemical accidents, volcanos, other scientific accidents, the production of artificial black holes, nanomachine infestations and quantum vacuum collapse. If one doesn't get you there are plenty more possibilities waiting in line...

Could it be that our lives are part of some grand design, by the One who has put us on an Earth uniquely designed to support us? If that is so then perhaps this *Intelligent Designer* doesn't want us to screw it all up, doesn't want us to blow ourselves up before we have fulfilled our potential.

Of course this is so. God is in full control of our lives, despite the machinations of the dictators, megalomaniacs, crazy scientists and Rogue States. He is in ultimate full control of history, even the stuff that hasn't happened yet. He has a glorious future for those who are His followers in this life, which reminds us of the incredible sacrifice that He made, spending thirty odd years in this evil, tainted, dysfunctional World, for the sole purpose of redeeming evil, tainted, dysfunctional mankind.

Perhaps you still need convincing. It is time to widen the discussion.

You may have noticed that, unlike most other books dealing with this subject, I haven't sprinkled the pages with Bible verses, to illustrate the points made. There's a good reason for this.

You have possibly never read the Bible before and probably have never held it in high esteem. You also would need some convincing that the Bible is *divinely* authored, so, if you were suddenly hit with, *the Bible says this* and the *Bible says that*, your first response would probably be, *so what?* In the eyes of non-Christians, the Bible has no more authority than any other book, whether religious tomes such as *the Koran,* or philosophic works such as *Das Kapital*, or even *Mein Kampf*, as an extreme example.

So, before I can quote from it authoritatively as the "Word of God", I should at least make some sort of case for it. After all, it's got a lot to live up to, especially when I say that I believe that every word in the Bible (in its original languages of Hebrew, Aramaic and Greek) is inspired by God, even though it has been authored by men (about 40 of them). This I take by faith and ultimately that is the challenge for us all.

How does that work then? No idea really, but God knows and that's good enough for me. But what a book! It was written over a 1500 year period, by people from a variety of backgrounds, written on three continents at times of war and times of peace, in three languages, yet it has as much relevance to us now as it had to its original readers. It comprises a variety of writing styles and genres, from poetry to history and has been translated more times than any other book, into over 240 languages and dialects.

The Bible is a magical book, not a book of magic. It is a timeless classic, full of human stories that address the problems of mankind in the 21st Century. We have enough lust, envy, jealousy and pride in the Bible to excite the palate of the most rabid soap fan. The Bible has the love stories and the triumphs against all the odds to warm the hearts of the most romantic fiction devotees. And there's sufficient blood, violence and retribution to excite the passions of... well, there's a bit of blood and, although it's not always in the best possible taste, it's there for a reason. That's the point of the Bible, everything is there for a reason, because there is *one* author, God Himself, and He sure knows how to write a book!

The celebrated French atheist, Voltaire, once declared that Christianity and the Bible would be extinct in a hundred years, yet only fifty years after his own extinction, his very house (where he made that declaration) was used by the Geneva Bible Society to print and store... Bibles. God always has the last laugh, just make sure that – unlike Voltaire – it's not at your expense!

One accusation thrown at Christians regarding the Bible is how it can possibly have remained intact, unadulterated, for so many centuries. *Surely it has been altered, air-brushed, to cover up the cracks of being disproved by historical events, to make its prophecies self-fulfilling and to correct its mistakes?* This is a favourite accusation from the Muslim World. Let me tell you a story.

Although the Bible concerns itself with events up until the middle of the 1st Century AD, the whole book wasn't gathered together in its finished state until at least 400 years later. So, realistically, there's plenty of scope for meddling with the words, particularly as it was describing events that happened centuries earlier.

Surely, if that can be proved, then the whole thing will come tumbling down.

The fact is that, if the atheists were able to present any evidence of this, then they would have done so by now. In 1947, it seemed, the issue could be settled there and then. In a cave near the Dead Sea, a shepherd boy happened to find jars containing old leather rolls. He did not know what they were, and sold them for next to nothing. Eventually archaeologists heard about the find and where it had been made. Between them, shepherds and archaeologists collected pieces of over 400 rolls. These books belonged to the library of a religious commune at Qumran, on the edge of the Dead Sea and the dry heat of the region preserved them. Their owners had hidden them in caves when the Roman army advanced against the rebel Jews in 68 AD. Every book of the Old Testament of the Bible is represented in this library, except the Book of Esther. These, of course, were the *Dead Sea Scrolls*.

In the Dead Sea Scrolls they found a complete Book of Isaiah, one of the largest books in the Old Testament and one of the most controversial in terms of content, because of the prophecies it contained, concerning the promised Messiah, the future of the Jewish people and also the fate of prominent cities, such as Petra and Babylon.

So here we are. The earliest complete book of Isaiah available before that time was dated at around 900 AD, but this copy, discovered among the Dead Sea Scrolls, was dated at around 100 BC. It was therefore around a thousand years older than any other Book of Isaiah known to man.

So, if there had been any tampering with the words during that thousand years, a time when Jesus walked this earth and fulfilled many of the prophecies in Isaiah, *then this would now be known*. Let the battle commence.

The text in the Isaiah scroll was word-for-word identical with over 95% of the text that appears in our current Bibles. Of the few variations, they were mainly slight spelling alterations and it must be stressed there were *no deviations in any of the key passages*. This is incredible when you think how many times this book was copied by scribes over that thousand year period and is revealing when you realise that there was no tampering with the text to fit in with historical occurrences.

So, when Jesus is described in Isaiah 53, centuries before he came, then this wasn't added *after the event*. When the Jews are described in Isaiah 43 as a people scattered to far-off lands, then this wasn't added *when they were scattered to far-off lands*. When the thriving city of Petra was condemned to desolation in Isaiah 34, then this wasn't added *when the city fell into ruins and has remained so ever since*. A similar story with Babylon in Isaiah 13.

Let us also consider the New Testament, which was originally written in Greek. There are, in fact, at least eight times as many surviving manuscripts of the New Testament than for any other ancient documents you may mention, such as Homer's *Iliad*. So we can safely say that the New Testament has come to us as an authentic document. In fact there are over 24,000 copies of original manuscripts and, guess what, they *all* agree with each other. The New Testament we read now is *exactly the same* as that originally written nearly 2000 years ago.

You've got to believe it, this Bible is special. There is no room here to pile on all other evidences, from history and archaeology, but, suffice it to say, there's plenty of it. All faith-building, but none of it a substitute for the real thing, *faith itself*. Faith, as I said, is the evidence of that not seen. We don't need proofs, but they are welcome additions to give extra credence to our beliefs.

Here's another one. There's a huge compendium of Jewish writings called the Talmud. Within its pages is an interesting report concerning the Temple in Jerusalem in the 1st Century AD. Once a year on *Yom Kippur* (The Day of Atonement) a scarlet cord would be tied to the horn of the scapegoat as the High Priest entered the Temple to make his annual sacrifice for the sins of the people. Every year this cord would miraculously turn white, indicating God's acceptance of this sacrifice. Yet, something strange happened one Yom Kippur, according to the Talmud. *"Our Rabbis taught: During the last forty years before the destruction of the Temple the lot did not come up in the right hand; nor did the crimson-coloured strap become white"*.

The Temple was destroyed in 70 AD. Forty years before this would be 30 AD. So, from 30 AD, God showed His displeasure by not accepting the annual Temple sacrifice for the forgiveness of the sins of the Jewish people. So what could have happened around 30 AD to incur divine annoyance? What single event did away with the need for further sacrifices, so much so, that any attempt at doing so would be rejected? Mmm, wasn't that the approximate date for the crucifixion of Jesus?

What is remarkable is that this could not be a contrived addition after the event as the last thing that the Jewish authors of the Talmud wanted to do was give credence to the claims of Jesus. Yet, there it was, within the pages of their writings.

So now you have more to think about. Perhaps it is time for you to make a decision or at least consider the implications of such a decision.

In the next two Chapters, we will examine such possibilities.

10 *Someone Saved My Life, That's Right*

Just think... you can finally satisfy *the Longing* that burns within you. You could live your life knowing that every second of it has real purpose, knowing that there can be real meaning in the madness that surrounds you and knowing that you can make a real difference to those around you. You could know that even when you screw up, there's a way back and that it matters not a jot what your background is... this is a genuine new start, strings attached. You could know that it matters not a fig whether you are a school kid in the playground, or a great grandfather in a retirement home, or whether you are born a Jew, Muslim, Catholic, Buddhist or a Cosmic Sojourner. It wouldn't matter whether you are man or woman, whether you were born with a silver spoon or a wooden spoon in your mouth. No qualifications are needed. We shall call this new life by the name of... *New Life*. It is the ultimate goal of *the Longing*.

You probably spotted the *strings attached* bit and first thought it was a slip of the pen, then thought, *he's slipped it in to trick me*. Well, cynical old you! In fact, you're right, there *are* strings attached. But they are not strings that can choke you, neither are they the strings of a puppet. Keep those strings in mind as we continue to imagine …

For every second of *New Life* you are not alone. Whatever may happen to you, good or bad, there is an unseen presence encouraging you, correcting you, even carrying you. It's not a dominant presence, in fact most of the time you are not even aware of it. It only rises to the surface of your attention when you ask or when you need it to. It is gentle and will go away if you ask it to. It is not a crutch for the weak, but rather a clutch to help you slip through the gears of life. It doesn't guarantee you a life without pain, or a life of material prosperity because it doesn't cocoon you from the troubles of the World. Instead it stands beside you through life's trials, helping you to navigate through life's minefields without fear. It demands only one thing from you, a sacrifice. Store that fact away as we imagine …

In *New Life*, you are encouraged to develop into a well rounded individual and you are even given help in this process. An instruction manual is provided, as well as a hot-line to a 24/7 celestial call centre. If applicable, special spiritual gifts are given to help you on your journey, gifts to use for others, both those who have already joined you on this exciting journey and those who are being urged to join up. You are never left helpless and are given all you need to deal with all that is thrown your way. You are even given the keys to an understanding of Life, the Universe and everything.

Oh yes, one last thing. You are granted the privilege of living forever after death, not as an ethereal being floating in the clouds playing the harp, but in purposeful, respectful and enjoyable employment.

And it may be a battered old cliché, but the surest thing about life is death. It's the only 100% probability in life, the fact that, someday, it's going to end. And it's not something you or your loved ones can plan for. Ask the friends and family of Robin Cook, who died suddenly and unexpectedly on holiday. A politician of massive intellect with a bright past and a brighter future died in his prime through a heart defect. Potential does not guarantee immortality, but the *New Life* does.

Does it sound a good deal? Too good to be true? It must be, otherwise we'd all be living *New Life*, wouldn't we? In an ideal World we would, but it's not an ideal World, so we don't. What, then, are the obstacles to living this life?

But, oh yes, I mentioned a downside, the *strings attached*. The word used was *sacrifice*. You're not getting a free lunch here, there needs to be some give and take. *New Life* doesn't just provide you with a toggle switch, where the act of flicking it to the 'On' position is the only effort needed on your part. No sirree Bob! *Sacrifice*.

But didn't you say earlier that God does not require any sacrifices any more, that Jesus ushered in a new way. Yes, he did, but sacrifice isn't just about blood-letting.

The first aspect of sacrifice concerns the World in which we live. The *New Life* declares that it may be *in* the World but not *of* the World. So it doesn't take you into an airy fairy place, where you avoid all contact with *Old Lifers*. Instead, you go about your business as before, but the sacrifice is in your actions, because you don't continue to do the same stuff.

The World glitters and flatters to deceive. It offers us bright lights, fun, excitement and entertainment. All we need to give is eight hours a day pen pushing, keyboard rattling or paper shifting if your collar is white, or a bit more muscle flexing if your collar is blue. In return the rest of the day is yours to spend, spend, spend or live, live, live or enjoy, enjoy, enjoy. This begins to be seen as a hollow existence.

New Life encourages you to ask some questions. Does money bring happiness? Do I need to be in a position of power or influence? Is sex alright between consenting adults? Too much money and life can just lose its challenge, with everything on a plate, leading to boredom, leading to drugs, alcohol, over eating... and an early grave! Too much power can leave you a very lonely person, surrounded by people who fear you, but not many who truly love you. Sex outside of a stable relationship can bring much grief, as your daily soaps can tell you.

New Life is encouraged by the words, "*I have come that they may have life, and have it to the full.*" These are not empty words or hopeful words. They are words of truth, spoken two thousand years ago by a man who, through his actions, brought the whole thing into play. And who is offering the *New Life*? Jesus Christ, of course, the same chap already mentioned in earlier Chapters.

The question that is most often asked is this: How on earth can the life of a man who lived two thousand years ago make a jot of a difference to someone living in the 21st Century? It's crazy, isn't it? But read this anonymous essay, written some years ago:

> *"Here is a man who was born in an obscure village, the child of a peasant woman. He grew up in another village. He worked in a carpenter shop until he was thirty, and then for three years he was an itinerant preacher. He never owned a home. He never wrote a book. He never held an office. He never had a family. He never went to college. He never put his foot inside a big city. He never travelled more than two hundred miles from the place where he was born. He never did one of the things that usually accompany greatness. He had no credentials but himself... I am far within the mark when I say that all the armies that ever marched, all the navies that ever were built; all the parliaments that ever sat and all the kings that ever reigned, put together, have not affected the life of man*

> *upon this earth as powerfully as has that one*
> *solitary life."*

There's something awesome about that one solitary life. There's definitely something going on here. We've been told about his death, but what of his life? The *New Life*, the *Christian* life is all about one man, not a religious system, not a list of do's and do-nots. One man – Jesus. Let's break this essay down:

> *Here is a man who was born in an obscure*
> *village, the child of a peasant woman.*

It was hardly an auspicious start in life. He was born in a stable because no rooms were available in the Bethlehem inns and motels. A home birth in Nazareth was out of the question because his parents were on government business and one tended not to question decisions of the Romans, who were the rulers of the land at that time. Because his father, Joseph, was a descendant of King David, Bethlehem was where they needed to be to register for the census. The irony was that Joseph wasn't even his real father, though he was also descended from King David through his mother, so the census was not entirely inaccurate. So what went on the census form? Father's name? *God*. Pardon me?

That's right, one half of Jesus' genes were from his mother, Mary, but the other half were pure divine stock.

The virgin birth meant that Joseph had no part in the proceedings, a fact that could have resulted in a stoning for Mary, as her pregnancy showed while she was still unmarried and standards of sexual morality were a lot more stringent in those days. So Jesus was born in Bethlehem, which was interesting because, hundreds of years earlier, the Biblical prophet Micah spoke of it,

"but you, Bethlehem Ephrathah, though you are small among the clans of Judah, out of you will come for me one who will be ruler over Israel, whose origins are from of old, from ancient times."

(Micah 5:2)

He grew up in another village.

Nazareth was his home village. It was a nondescript place in the north of the land, in the Galilee region, where the family of Jesus settled after a brief interlude in Egypt, to which they fled due to the actions of the deranged and paranoid King Herod. Although only a puppet monarch of the Romans, when he heard of the birth of Jesus in fulfillment of numerous prophecies, he went berserk and ordered the death of all infant boys in the area of Bethlehem, where the family were living at the time. Jesus only just escaped in time and stayed in Egypt until Herod died, possibly of gangrene of the private parts, a fitting end to a madman. They returned to Nazareth, where Jesus grew up, *in wisdom and stature.*

He worked in a carpenter shop until he
was thirty,

Many legends have been bandied about of weird and wonderful miracles attributed to Jesus while he was growing up, usually involving talking to the animals a la Doctor Doolittle. But the fact is that the Bible is silent on these years, as shall I be, except to say that he would have had a typical, unspectacular Jewish upbringing and helped his "dad" out in the family trade, as would any son.

and then for three years he was an
itinerant preacher.

It's incredible to think that all the events of Jesus' life, his teachings, miracles and more, were sandwiched into three years, the final years, of his life. Think back to exactly three years ago, make a mental mark and then list all that you have accomplished since then. Now measure that up against the recorded events in his life, bearing in mind the admission of one of his biographers, John, who said, *Jesus did many other things as well. If every one of them were written down, I suppose that even the whole world would not have room for the books that would be written.* Here's a partial list:

There were nine miracles, from stilling of storms, feeding lots of people, to walking on water and turning water into wine. There were twenty major healings of diseases, including leprosy, paralysis, blindness, epilepsy, deafness and a missing ear. Three people were brought back to life. Four people delivered of demonic possession. Then there was his teaching. In many ways he wasn't teaching anything new, except when he spoke of himself and of things yet to happen in the World. It was the way that he explained things, expressing concepts in fresh relevant ways, using word pictures, familiar stories and direct exposition, that made his teaching remarkable. The Lord's Prayer, that he taught his friends, is still well-known, even to non-Christians and the Sermon on the Mount still remains as a standard of human behaviour that is often striven for but never attained.

He never owned a home.

His mission kept him on the move. He tended to pay visits on people, through his travels. Some offered him a temporary base. There are no accounts of him inviting others for a fireside chat in any home owned by himself, or his family.

He never wrote a book.

He didn't need to, there was no time. It was up to others to put things down on paper (or, rather, manuscript). He surrounded himself with twelve special helpers, disciples. Two of them, Matthew and John, kept eye-witness records of the remarkable events of his life. Others kept their eyes open too and, no doubt, provided the material for the other two chroniclers of his life, Mark and Luke. These four books form the *Gospels*, the first four books of the New Testament.

He never held an office.

That came later, with myriads of titles Christians have granted themselves and others. Just looking at the Roman Catholic hierarchy, we have The Pope, cardinals, auxiliary bishops, priests, deacons and the rest. The C of E also has its archbishops, rectors, vicars, archdeacons, deans, canons and curates. These people would be known by such exalted titles as Reverend, Right Reverend, Most Reverend, Father, Excellency, even Your Holiness!

Jesus made do with the simpler, less grand title of *rabbi* or *teacher*. If there was an office for a teacher / miracle worker / saviour of mankind then he was your man for this unique role, but if there was to be a single title that would fit him best, the clue is in the name. His name was not Jesus, that is just the English translation of the Greek translation. His actual name was *Yeshua*, a Hebrew name, meaning *saviour*. The name says it all.

He never had a family.

He had a mum and his (real) dad was not of this World. He also had four brothers. But despite the money-spinning musings of millionaire Dan Brown (in *The Da Vinci Code*), there is absolutely no truth (but great profit) in the theory that Jesus married Mary Magdelene and founded a dynasty. Jesus was unique. He was cut off in his prime, such was the sad demand of his mission on Earth. At one point he was asked about his mother and his brothers and he said *who is my mother and who are my brothers?* Pointing to his close friends, he said, *these are my mother and brothers.* He belonged to the World, in particular to those who followed him and believed in him. *Whoever does the will of God is my brother and sister and mother*, he added.

He never went to college.

Not a qualification to his name, not even a GCSE level in woodwork, though there's no doubt he was capable of attaining this level. He was schooled, as was any Jewish male of his time, in the Hebrew Scriptures, the words that we know as the Old Testament of The Bible. Much of it would have been committed to heart, as would have many of the Oral traditions passed down from teachers of old.

He never put his foot inside a big city.

Well there weren't any in Israel at that time!

He never travelled more than two hundred miles from the place where he was born.

He never made any overseas trips. His feet probably *didn't* walk upon "England's mountains green". In his three years of mission, he trod the highways and byways of Ancient Israel, visiting and revisiting many places. As he once said that his mission was to the Jewish people, then his travels were consistent with this idea. Although popular with the common people, the Jewish establishment were deeply suspicious of him and plotted his ultimate downfall. He had very few interactions with non-Jews, the most telling being at the end of his life, dying at the hands of Roman soldiers.

He never did one of the things that usually accompany greatness.

An interesting statement. Greatness in our World, when attributed to individuals, tends to be showered on those who have created great military empires, such as Alexander *the Great*, Peter *the Great* or Catherine *the Great*. None of them were paragons of virtue, far from it, particularly in the case of Catherine, who was a royal nymphomaniac.

Greatness also seems to conjure up such qualities as nobility, power, eminence, grand and distinguished. Ironically, these are words that may come to mind if you venture into Westminster Abbey or the Sistine Chapel, places dripping with the trappings of power and eminence etc. Arguably, Jesus wouldn't set foot in any of these places created in his honour, his kind of greatness was far different. His greatness was expressed in humility, righteousness and morality a far cry from the world of Alexander, Peter and Catherine.

He had no credentials but himself...

This is a most telling statement because the most important thing about Jesus is not his teachings or miracles, but who he claimed to be. He made these claims throughout his three years and it was these claims that eventually did for him. The key to this is given in the following exchange between Jesus and the religious authorities at his trial near the end of his life:

> *"Again the high priest asked him, "Are you the Christ, the Son of the Blessed One?"*
>
> *"I am," said Jesus. "And you will see the Son of Man sitting at the right hand of the Mighty One and coming on the clouds of heaven." The high priest tore his clothes. "Why do we need any more witnesses?" he asked. "You have heard the blasphemy. What do you think?" They all condemned him as worthy of death".*

(Mark 14:61-64)

He could have saved his own life if he'd kept quiet, but his credentials *had* to be expressed, it was the whole point of his mission. His miracles were to get people to sit up and notice, his teachings were to show people how to live their lives and how to know God better. But what he said about himself was what it was all about.

He was the Christ, the Messiah, the Son of Man and much more. In fact there are over 100 titles given to Jesus, all taken from The Bible. But the key title and the most common one is *The Christ*. This comes from the Greek translation of the Hebrew word, *Messiah*, which means 'anointed one', a special person earmarked by God for a special purpose.

The final paragraph of that anonymous essay surely speaks for itself.

> *I am far within the mark when I say that all the armies that ever marched, all the navies that ever were built; all the parliaments that ever sat and all the kings that ever reigned, put together, have not affected the life of man upon this earth as powerfully as has that one solitary life.*

This is who we Christians follow.

11 *The End (or is it The Beginning)*

This is it, the bottom line. Take it or leave it.

Jesus, the Messiah, the Saviour, the Christ, interrupted his life in eternity, in heaven, or whatever you call the place where God is, to live on Earth, to give us those marvellous teachings, to set such a wonderful example but, most of all, to die.

Remember what we learned earlier. The sacrificial system, instituted by God, was the only means of man getting right with Him. Without the shedding of the blood of an innocent, there can be no way back to Him because our sins and misdemeanours get in the way and our imperfections can't live with the perfection of the Creator and Sustainer of the Universe.

Here's where the two worlds collide.

Man, racked by sin and guilt is unable to find true communion with God, his heavenly father. There are too many sins with too many blood sacrifices needed to cover them and no other way to find peace with his Creator. Yet he has *the Longing* in his heart …

God, motivated by love and compassion, reaches down to man and offers a full reconciliation by offering Himself, as the Jesus of history, the man who lived among us and gave us a glimpse of God himself, as… a *sacrifice*.

He took the place of all those animals slaughtered in the Temple and he allowed himself to be captured, tried by the Jewish court for blasphemy and executed by the Romans. Death was by crucifixion, death on a cross. A Bible quote seems apt at this point:

*"This is love: not that we loved God, but that he
loved us and sent his Son as an atoning sacrifice for
our sins."*

(1 John 4:10)

Such a death. This wasn't Hitler, Stalin or Saddam Hussein, who deserved it. This wasn't your average thief, villain or scoundrel who probably deserved it. This was a person who was present at the Creation of the Universe, who could have called a legion of angels to stop what was happening, who had the choice to do what he wanted. He chose his death, he chose *such a death!*

So what can I do, already?

To become a child of God, a beneficiary of the *New Life*, one has to do two things. Firstly …

Jesus needs to be "received".

Many of us live in a box of our own making, our *personal space*. This space includes all that is necessary for daily life and makes us comfortable. In it we find our workplace, our family, friends, our bed, perhaps an iPod, mobile phone and PC. If all outside the box ceased to exist then we could still carry on with life and perhaps, if some of us are honest, things might even improve. To be frank, this is no way to live. It restricts us to the parameters we set for ourselves, it discourages us from interacting with the World at large and it totally unprepares us for the unexpected.

For us to have any chance for this New Life, then we must tear down the walls of our box and allow Jesus to enter. What does this mean? It's not just to believe what Jesus has done, we need to make it personal. It's not just head knowledge, it's heart action that is needed. We have to respond, we have to be willing to go where we're taken by this new knowledge. Theory must become practice. But, before this can happen, there's the second thing we must do …

Jesus needs to be "believed".

We are ready to receive, we're in the right frame of mind. Now there's the simple matter of believing it all. It's all or nothing, the New Life is not pick and mix. Jesus was a good man and a great teacher, *but* he also claimed to be God himself. Jesus died a horrific death by crucifixion *but* he returned to life three days later. These *buts* are vitally important because they are as much a part of the complete picture as what came before them.

There is only one way we can accept these *buts*, in fact only one way that we can receive this *New Life*. It's that *F* word again. We need *faith*!

No-one has all the answers. If you're the type of person who has 1001 (or even 101) questions that have to be answered before you would even contemplate investigating the claims of Jesus, then you're still living firmly in your box, ready to repel all boarders! It is true that Christianity provokes as many questions as answers. This is why faith is needed. It's a sacrifice, it's showing trust in the unseen. It's not easy. In our society we are taught to expect to understand everything and to be suspicious of everything we can't see or touch.

Even Christians who have been in the *New Life* for years still need to exercise their faith muscles. But it's different for them, because they have someone they can ask. They have uncovered the mother lode, and discovered that faith is actually a gift from God with the more you ask for, the more you receive. But you have to make the first move and the greatest act of faith you'll ever make is right now. This is because your brain is now telling you, *what on earth are you asking me to believe?*

I believe that, even in this small book, there are sufficient raw facts for you to act on, but even then I urge you to read one of Jesus' biographies in the New Testament. Try the book of Mark, it's the shortest and the fastest moving. You can read it in a couple of hours and it will give you a well-rounded insight into the life and times of Jesus.

There's so much to understand, but, if our mortal minds, constrained by the grey matter in our brain, were capable of understanding the *deeper things* then we're putting ourselves on par with God, which is ridiculous. That would be a God made in our image, not the God that I know. Be comforted by the fact that God will give you all the faith you need once you have made the first step.

Understanding Him is a lifelong task for Christians and for all of us. We don't get the full picture until we see Him face to face in heaven. What we need to do, in this first step, is to admit that we don't know everything and that we are willing to accept, by faith, the basic facts that would lead us into the *New Life* and hold onto the promise that, in the incredible journey that lies ahead, other parts of the jigsaw will begin to fall into place.

So what now? Well we start by contemplating our navels. Not literally, of course, it's not physical fluff we must first deal with, but a different kind of fluff. We need a long hard look at the bits of fluff in our lives that have clogged things up. All the times we have stuffed up, when we've done something we ought not to have done, or when we haven't done something we ought to have done. Close your eyes, mutter a little prayer of help and, believe me, there will be a tailback of images in your mind's eye. Pay particular attention to people you have hurt in any way, either through intent or negligence.

Now hold that thought and focus on a new word, another maligned word from the Christian lexicon, to rank alongside "sin" in the Top Ten of neglected terms. The new word is *repentance*. What does that conjure up? Wild eyed men with spittle in their beards and venom in their words, parading where they're not wanted and preaching judgement, hell and brimstone? Perhaps a negative view, but not a negative word, because it's a word describing an action with a very positive outcome. This is what Jesus had to say about it.

> *"The time has come," he said. "The kingdom of God is near. Repent and believe the good news!"*

(Mark 1:15)

So, flipping our minds back to our *crimes and misdemeanours*, it's not just enough to remember them, it's to acknowledge that our actions were less than perfect, to say sorry for them to God and, where possible, to make a decision to get right with all who you have wronged, when the occasion arises. Did I say this is easy? Well it ain't, but rest assured there will be help on the way. This is what repenting is and it also implies, naturally, making a real effort not to repeat your mistakes (or sins).

In the above quote we see repeated what was mentioned in the first quote. Receive and *believe*, repent and *believe*. It's easy... and it's hard. It's easy because *externally* it's only a matter of saying words. It's hard because *internally* it requires a complete change of heart, a willingness to admit your sins and your need for God in your life to walk alongside you.

And it's all focused on Jesus and his death on the cross. The fact is that he didn't just die for Christians, but he died for all of mankind who receive and believe. He died for mass murderers, he died for wife beaters, he died for World leaders. All are equal when it comes to this offer, but the reality is that it is only Christians who gain the benefit, if you think about it.

Only Christians, thankful for the *New Life* that lives within them, acknowledge what Jesus has done, that is why they are Christians, by definition! You've got to join the club if you want the shiny badge! Everyone else is just a *potential* Christian, unaware or not bothered about the riches that lie within their grasp. Where do you stand? Do you wish to go further? If, so then read on.

These are the sort of words that should leave your lips or enter your thoughts at this stage:

> *I am prepared to believe that Jesus Christ,*
> *the Son of God, came into this world to die*
> *and take away my sins, providing the way*
> *for a relationship between myself and God,*
> *my creator.*

That's all you need to do for starters. It's not a formula, you can say it in your own words, just follow the gist. The key is to mean what you say, not to say it as a spell that unlocks heavenly power. Remember, you are speaking to a real Person, and it's a relationship you are asking for, not a legal contract.

But there's still the matter of that tailback of crimes and misdemeanours, sins that you have committed and perhaps still plan to commit. It's time to deal with those. But it's not one-way traffic, because God has made you a promise concerning them.

> *"If we confess our sins, he is faithful and just*
> *and will forgive us our sins and purify us from*
> *all unrighteousness".*

(1 John 1:9)

It's called assurance of forgiveness and it is truly awesome. Because God never lies and He has given us His assurance that, because of what Jesus did for us on the cross, *all* our sins will be forgiven. From God's point of view, nothing you have done in the past will be held against you any more. As far as He's concerned, the slate is wiped clean.

Now that may be OK with God, but there's still a question of those you have upset, attacked, spoken against and disrespected in the past. As a consequence of your decision, a few bridges may have to be rebuilt and more than a few wrongs will need to be righted. And, of course, you're going to have to do your best to make sure you don't continue to upset, attack, speak against and disrespect etc.

God assures you that all of your sins, however bad, can be forgiven. All you have to do is ask. Work through your crimes and misdemeanours and, in each case, be honest before God when you feel personal responsibility. Just say sorry, mean what you say, then move on.

The *New Life* is so close now, you can almost touch it. More words from Jesus:

> *"I tell you the truth, whoever hears my word and*
> *believes him who sent me has eternal life and will not be*
> *condemned; he has crossed over from death to life".*
>
> (John 5:24)

The death of Jesus was not the end of *his* story – it was the beginning of *history*, because, just two days later, Jesus came back to life. He had cheated death, he was resurrected. He lives forever – and so can we.

The *New Life* is not just about a new life of purpose and meaning in this World, it's all that and eternal life too! What a gift!

You may (or may not) have prayed that prayer I suggested a little earlier. It was just a little one, to dust away the cobwebs and get you in the right frame of mind. After all, disregarding a desperate dart launched heavenwards on behalf of your football team, you probably haven't prayed since you were a kid! That was just an opener. Next I urged you to work through the bad stuff in your life in honest repentance for your sins, with a decision to do your level best not to repeat them. Finally, the big one, the clincher.

If you feel ready, then I suggest that, in an attitude of honesty, you get your brain in gear and say the following:

> *"Lord Jesus, I admit that I have been living
> a life away from you and I am really sorry.
> I believe that you died so that I may be
> forgiven for all my sins. Please forgive me
> now. Please come into my life by your Holy
> Spirit and help me to live a life that would be
> pleasing to you. Amen."*

As before, it's not a secret formula, or invocation, you're not forcing God into a contract, you're simply knocking on the door to heaven. And you're making right use of the *F* word.

Welcome to the *New Life*.

This is just the beginning… ask God to show you what comes next.

Reading list

Before you read anything else I urge you to get yourself a copy of the Bible (I prefer the New King James Version) and immerse yourself in it. As I said earlier, it's no ordinary book, it's a conduit between God and man, so why not first ask God to illuminate your way.

Just to get started, I recommend flipping through these five books of the Old Testament and the New Testament, to get an overview of the whole story.

Old Testament

1. Genesis – to give you the foundations (as well as a rollicking good read).

2. Exodus – to show how the nation of Israel was forged.

3. Judges – to explore the seeds of Israel's downfall.

4. Jeremiah – Chapters 1-7 – to watch the unravelling of the nation.

5. Isaiah – Chapters 9 and 52-55 – to read about the promised future deliverer and king.

New Testament

1. Matthew – to explain the life and mission of Jesus, the deliverer and king.

2. John – a wordier and more thoughtful account of the life and mission of Jesus.

3. Acts – to marvel at the life and times of the early Church.

4. Romans – to understand the implications of what Jesus did and the benefits of the New Life.

5. Ephesians – to understand what a Church should be.

When you have done that, start again and read the whole Bible ☺ in its entirety.

If you have any questions on what you've read, send them to me at www.sppublishing.com and hopefully I can either answer them or direct you to others who can help you.